# automobiles
of
america

# automobiles
# of
# america

by
automobile manufacturers association, inc.

a savoyard book
detroit ● wayne state university press ● 1968

Library of Congress Catalog Card No. 68-29740

Second, revised edition © 1968 by
AUTOMOBILE MANUFACTURERS ASSOCIATION, INC.

Published by the Wayne State University Press, Detroit, Michigan 48202. Published simultaneously in Canada by Ambassador Books, Limited, Rexdale, Ontario, Canada.

# contents

Foreword, 5

Acknowledgments, 9

Milestones, 11

Pioneers, 179

Roll Call, 203

Highlights, 249

Index, 257

# foreword

In the waning years of the 19th century a new age dawned —the age of the automobile.

The distribution of the world's automobiles today would indicate that the dawn's first light was seen in America. But this was not so. While no other country in the world has approached the United States in the production and use of automobiles, the indomitable machine that has revolutionized our way of life was born in Europe.

Actually, however, the automobile was not "born" in the sense of being invented by anyone. It is the product of an evolutionary process that started long before mankind ever dreamed of such a thing as an "auto age."

Automobile history can be traced to the time of Leonardo da Vinci or even as far back as the discovery of the wheel. Historians set 1769 as the year of the first self-propelled land vehicle—a cumbersome steam artillery tractor built by French Army Captain Nicolas Cugnot. In 1805, a mobile steam dredge was produced by Oliver Evans of Philadelphia. And during the first half of the last century, steam powered carriages actually were in operation on the roads of England.

But the mechanical evolution of the modern automobile really began to take form about 100 years ago when European inventors such as Eugene Langen and Nikolaus August Otto developed the internal combustion engine.

It was 1864 when Langen and Otto formed a company to produce and sell their revolutionary power plants which ran on coal gas instead of steam. An Otto engine displayed at the Paris Exposition of 1867 attracted world-wide attention. In 1876, another Otto engine was shown at the Philadelphia Centennial Exposition, stirring further interest in this country.

By 1876 Otto had developed the four-cycle engine and in 1885 successfully operated an engine on liquid fuel.

In a few years, similar engines were being made in the United States as a new and attractive source of power for lumbering, pumping, power generation and marine uses. And it wasn't long before men were tinkering with the idea of using such an engine to propel a carriage.

In this application, however, the Europeans still were ahead. Vehicles operated by internal-combustion engines were built in the 1880's by Europeans Gottlieb Daimler, Karl Benz, Wilhelm Maybach, Emile Levassor and others. Daimler and Maybach were granted a German patent on a V-2 engine as early as June 9, 1889. These two also displayed a motor vehicle at the Paris Exposition of 1889.

By this time, the word "automobile" had not even been coined. But the idea of a practical self-propelled vehicle already had captured the imagination of many men, both in Europe and the United States. New names—some uncomplimentary—were invented for the new contraptions. "Horseless carriage" perhaps was the most common early term, and "gas buggy" was coined for the gas-burning internal-combustion variety. By the time the twentieth century was well into its first decade, the terms "automobile," or "auto" and "motor car," or "car," were the common expressions.

In the beginning the gasoline car was up against stiff competition from both steam and electric-powered makes. Ultimately, however, the internal-combustion engine emerged the winner.

When the automobile appeared on the U. S. scene it was somewhat like a ship on a desert. America was virtually a roadless land. By 1900, all of the hard-surfaced roads in the United States would not have linked New York and Boston.

A few carriage routes went beyond the cities and towns. But in wet weather they turned into winding rivers of mud. When dry, they were deeply rutted and dusty. Under any conditions, they offered little encouragement to pioneers of the dawning motor age.

But, the motoring enthusiasts of that early day were a hardy, adventurous lot. By 1903, one had even managed to drive an automobile from coast to coast, clear across the roadless land.

With such audacity, motorists themselves proved the practical potentialities of motor travel and led the way to better roads.

A mere *8,000* crude automobiles were chugging over dirt roads and cobblestone streets at the turn of the century. Today some *97.5* million motor vehicles of all types are in use, traveling *932* billion miles a year across *3.7* million miles of roads and streets.

The family car has become an American institution. *Four-fifths of American families* now own cars on which they depend for going to and from work, shopping, and such day-to-day necessities as taking children to school. More than *80 per cent* of vacation trips are made by car.

The automotive industry, to keep pace with the growing demand for motor vehicles, has produced more than *240 million* cars, trucks and buses. The ratio of motor vehicles to population has reached *1 to 2.2*.

Automobiles are directly responsible for the existence in the U. S. today of more than *three-quarters* of a million business enterprises—including many types and varieties never known before the "auto age." Automotive transportation industries provide jobs for more than *12* million people, or one in every seven employed in the country.

7

This infinitely flexible and individual form of transportation has changed virtually every aspect of American life —ending isolation both in the city and on the farm, stimulating development of the land and spearheading the growth of the nation's vigorous economy.

Through the pages that follow, the uniquely American phase of automotive history is told in four parts—(1) in "Milestones," a chronological review of significant events; (2) in "Pioneers," a selection of brief biographical sketches of outstanding leaders on America's automotive frontier; (3) in "Roll Call," a listing of the hundreds of American cars and trucks that have appeared through the years; (4) in "Highlights," a few basic facts and figures that tell more precisely than words how the automobile has affected Twentieth Century America.

AUTOMOBILE MANUFACTURERS ASSOCIATION, INC.

# acknowledgments

*Automobiles of America* was compiled and written largely from the wealth of historic source material—newspaper clippings, trade journals, catalogues, and books—available in the library of the Automobile Manufacturers Association, Inc. The "Milestones" section constitutes a revision and updating of a now out-of-print AMA publication, *A Chronicle of the Automotive Industry in America.*

Many individuals assisted in the preparation of this publication, but of noteworthy value were the contributions of the following:

Christy Borth, for editorial comments;

James J. Bradley, chief, Automotive History Collection, Detroit Public Library, for the index;

Harry N. Rogan, Automobile Club of Michigan, for his help with the "Roll Call;" and

Stanley K. Yost, for his critical reading of the early years.

The AMA collection of historic automotive photographs provided most of the illustrations. The following organizations also contributed:

Bureau of Public Roads

Detroit Public Library

Henry Ford Museum

Library of Congress

R. E. Olds Company

The Smithsonian Institution

9

1893—America's first workable gasoline-engine vehicle. Designed by Charles E. Duryea, built and driven by J. Frank Duryea.

# milestones

Along the ancient roadways of the world, milestones marked the slow progress of the traveler. And while modern America is transported more efficiently and guided by more elaborate road markers, the word "milestone" still stands for the mark of progress. To reach its present state of highway transportation efficiency, the nation had to pass many such milestones along the way. Below and on the following pages are listed many of the important milestones of automotive history in America.

## Early experiments

*1893* America's first successful gasoline-engine motor vehicle was in operation on Sept. 21 in Springfield, Mass. Using the designs of Charles E. Duryea, his brother J. Frank Duryea built a single-cylinder horseless carriage. The Duryea vehicle was the first American-made car to have an electric ignition and a spray carburetor, both of which J. Frank Duryea designed and built.

A national good roads movement sparked by cycling enthusiasts prompted establishment of the U. S. Office of Road Inquiry under the Department of Agriculture. This office later became the Bureau of Public Roads, under the Department of Commerce. The founding statute signed by President Benjamin Harrison read in part: "To enable the

Secretary of Agriculture to make inquiries in regard to the systems of road management throughout the United States, to make investigations in regard to the best methods of road-making, and to enable him to assist the agricultural college and experiment stations in disseminating information on this subject, ten thousand dollars."

The first brick surface on a rural road in the U. S. was laid on the Wooster Pike near Cleveland, Ohio. The four miles of brick pavement were completed in the fall of 1893 near route 71 of the Interstate Highway System.

*1894* A car conceived by Elwood G. Haynes of Kokomo, Ind., was constructed by Elmer and Edgar Apperson, assisted by Jonathan Dixon Maxwell. Powered by a one-cylinder engine, the 820-pound Haynes car operated on Pumpkinvine Pike in Kokomo on July 4th, at a speed of six miles per hour.

Edward Joel Pennington probably operated one of his cars this year—there were several in existence by 1895.

1894—Elwood Haynes in his first car. It was
powered by a single cylinder engine built by
Clark Sintz of Grand Rapids, Mich.

*1895* In September the first American company estab-
lished to make gasoline cars was the Duryea
Motor Wagon Company, organized by Charles E. and J.
Frank Duryea.

The U. S. Patent Office granted George Baldwin Selden
the patent he had applied for in 1879. The Selden Patent
covered the essential features of the modern gasoline automobile. Features of special significance were: an internal
combustion engine of the two-cycle type developed by
George B. Brayton using liquid hydrocarbon fuel with a
power shaft running faster than the road wheels, and a
clutch or disconnecting device between the engine and the
propelling wheels.

Hiram Percy Maxim started a motor carriage department
for Pope Mfg., Co., bicycle makers of Hartford, Conn.

The first U. S. motor vehicle race, in which any contes-
tants finished was sponsored by the Chicago Times-Herald
and run over a snow-drifted course in Chicago on Thanks-

1895—The patent granted to George Selden was regarded for many years master document, covering all the esse features of the gasoline automobile.

giving Day, Nov. 28, was won by J. Frank Duryea in a Duryea Motor Wagon at an average speed of 7½ miles per hour (considering delays for repairs) over the 55 mile course. Of the six starters, only two completed the run. Second place was won by a Mueller-Benz, driven across the finish line by Charles Brady King of Detroit, an umpire, who took over the tiller when driver Oscar Mueller collapsed from exposure an hour before the end of the race. The *Times-Herald* contest was scheduled to run on Nov. 1, but was postponed to allow entrants more time to prepare their vehicles. For those present and ready to compete the judges allowed a consolation race on Nov. 2 which was actually the first U. S. motor vehicle race. Four vehicles started, but breakdowns and accidents put all the vehicles out of the contest.

Public interest in horseless carriages heightened late in the year. The first American automotive trade journals started publication: "The Horseless Age," edited by E. P. Ingersoll of New York, and "The Motorcycle," edited by E. E. Goff of Chicago. In addition, the nation's first automotive association, the American Motor League, was organized in Chicago.

1895—The Duryea entry, winner of America's first motor vehicle race. J. Frank Duryea at the tiller, with Arthur W. White, umpire, of Toronto, as passenger.

## A new industry is born

*1896* J. Frank Duryea, as chief engineer of the Duryea Motor Wagon Company, produced a third car. From these plans 13 cars were built that year—the first time that more than one car was made from the same design in the U. S.

George H. Morill, Jr., of Norwood, Mass., bought one

1896—Henry Ford and his experimental "Quadricycle."

1896—The first gasoline powered car on the streets of Detroit. Charles B. King at the tiller, Oliver E. Barthel as passenger.

1896—America's first track race for motor vehicles—September at Narragansett Park, Cranston, R. I.

of the 13 Duryea Motor Wagons, and thus became the first known purchaser of an American gasoline car.

Charles Brady King drove the first car on the streets of Detroit, March 6. The car was powered with a four-cylinder, four-cycle, water-cooled engine that King designed and built.

Barnum & Bailey Circus announced an exhibition of the Duryea Motor Wagon as a parade feature on April 2.

Hiram Percy Maxim of the Pope Mfg. Co., in Hartford, Conn., built an electric motor carriage.

On Memorial Day, J. Frank Duryea won the Cosmopolitan Race (New York City to Irvington-on-the-Hudson and return). This was the third motor vehicle race in the U. S.

Henry Ford successfully operated his two-cylinder, four horsepower, "Quadricycle" in Detroit on June 4.

The French word, "automobile," first began to appear in published references to motor vehicles in the U. S.

America's first motor vehicle track races were run at Narragansett Park, R. I., on Sept. 7. Seven vehicles were entered, two electrics and five Duryeas, but two of the Duryeas were disqualified. All five heats, one mile each, were won by a Riker Electric Stanhope. Average for the first mile was 26.8 miles per hour. Second prize went to a Morris and Salom Electrobat. The race was so dull that spectators demanded, "Get a horse!" This was probably the origin of the famous phrase.

1896—Alexander Winton and five companions in his first experimental car.

Alexander Winton of Cleveland produced an experimental two-seater motor carriage in September.

During the same month, Ransom Eli Olds drove a one-cylinder, six horsepower car on the streets of Lansing, Mich. He had been experimenting with steam-powered vehicles since 1886.

Two Duryea cars participated in the Emancipation Day run from London to Brighton on Nov. 14. This event celebrated repeal of England's "red flag" laws, and marked the first appearance of American motor vehicles in Europe.

*1897* The first automotive press preview and open house in the U. S. was held at the Pope Mfg. Co., in Hartford, Conn., on May 13. Invitations were sent to journalists to see the Pope plant and try out the firm's automobiles.

1897—The Stanley twins in their famous Stanley Steamer.

A Winton car was driven a mile in one minute and 48 seconds in Cleveland (on Memorial Day), and from Cleveland to New York in 10 days (July 28–Aug. 7).

Olds Motor Vehicle Company was organized on Aug. 21 —the first automobile company in Michigan. Studebaker Brothers, carriage-makers since 1852, began experimenting with motor vehicles.

Louis S. Clarke and William Morgan of Pittsburgh, Pa., organized Pittsburgh Motor Vehicle Co., Oct. 21.

Pope Manufacturing Co., Hartford, Conn., began marketing Columbia Mark III Electric Phaetons.

Gilbert Loomis, a mechanic from Westfield, Mass., who built his own one-cylinder car, took out automobile insurance. The premium was $7.50 for $1,000 worth of liability insurance on a policy used for horse-drawn vehicle liability.

1898—Hiram Percy Maxim and Bert Holcomb in a Mark VIII Pope-Columbia.

*1898* William E. Metzger of Detroit established the first independent automotive dealership.

The earliest known franchised dealership for U. S. cars was opened by H. O. Koller in Reading, Pa., to sell Winton motor vehicles.

Electric cab service was initiated in New York City.

Haynes was the first U. S. motor vehicle manufacturer to use aluminum alloy.

Winton introduced a Commercial Delivery Wagon, and built a quantity of one-cylinder passenger cars.

John Wilkinson built his first four-cylinder, valve-in-head, air-cooled motor, from which Franklin engines later evolved.

*1899* Experiments in collecting mail with motor vehicles were conducted in Buffalo, Cleveland and Washington by the U. S. Post Office Department.

The Automobile Club of America was organized.

The U. S. Army purchased its first electric vehicles for general transportation assignments.

Alexander Winton drove one of his cars from Cleveland to New York in 47 hours and 37 minutes driving time.

R. E. Olds organized his second company, the Olds Motor Works, and moved operations from Lansing to Detroit.

A Haynes-Apperson car was delivered from the factory in Kokomo, Ind., to Brooklyn in 21 days.

Electric delivery wagons were put into use by New York and Boston stores.

Freelan O. Stanley, driving a Stanley Steamer built by himself and his twin brother, Francis E., climbed Mt. Washington, N. H., in August.

Rollin White adopted the flash boiler, developed in Europe, for experiments with steam cars.

A. L. Dyke of St. Louis, Mo., established the first automobile parts and supply business in the U. S.

Mrs. John Howell Phillips of Chicago was the first woman known in the U. S. to receive a driver's license.

American Motor Company, New York City, opened a garage with "competent mechanics always on hand to make repairs when necessary."

Pittsburgh Motor Vehicle Company became the Autocar Company on Aug. 28.

Percy Owen opened the first automobile salesroom in New York City at 120 Broadway, on Nov. 1. The firm sold Winton cars.

James Ward Packard completed and ran his first car in Warren, Ohio on Nov. 6. With his brother, Warren D., and George L. Weiss, of Cleveland as partners, he formed the New York and Ohio Co., to build the Packard car.

Back Bay Cycle & Motor Company of Boston, opened a stable for "renting, sales, storage and repair of motor vehicles."

The Stanley Brothers sold their steam car rights to Mobile and Locomobile.

"Motor Age" published its first issue in September.

1899—The Mobile Steamer had center steering because it was felt the car could be controlled more easily.

21

*1900* The First National Automobile Show was held Nov. 3–10 in New York City's Madison Square Garden under the sponsorship of the Automobile Club of America. An estimated 48,000 visitors saw displays by 40 automobile and 11 parts and accessory exhibitors. There were about 300 types of vehicles exhibited, with prices ranging from $280 to $4,000. The exhibits were valued at $565,000. The Mobile Company of America built a 200-foot

1900—First National Automobile Show at New York's old Madison Square Garden featured test drives on obstacle courses.

ramp extending 53 feet in height to the Garden roof for demonstrating the hill climbing ability and good brakes of the steamers.

Mack introduced a bus which ran eight years as a bus and was then converted into a truck, to run nine more years.

1900—The first truck built by White was a steamer which introduced "horseless" delivery service.

President McKinley was the first U. S. President to ride in an automobile.

New York City acquired a motor-driven ambulance.

The Saturday Evening Post carried its first automobile advertising.

The publication "Automobile Topics" made its appearance.

Gasoline engines were located under a hood for the first time in the U. S. by several American automobile manufacturers.

John Brisben Walker drove his steam car to the top of Pikes Peak.

Special kerosene lamps for automobiles were offered by the R. E. Dietz Co., New York City, featuring a 20 candlepower reflected clear white flame capable of casting a 200-foot beam. One of the primary advantages of the Dietz lamp was that it produced a steady light even over rough roads.

A gasoline car defeated electric and steam cars for the first time in a free-for-all race at Washington Park race track in Chicago.

Engineer's certificates were issued by New York City as drivers' licenses. Harold T. Birnie was the first to receive one of these driving permits on May 15.

23

Carl Breer at the age of 17 built his first motor vehicle. (Later Breer was one of the engineers for the first Chrysler car.)

The National Association of Automobile Manufacturers was organized.

The G & J, designed by Thomas Jeffery, was the forerunner of the Rambler—the car had the engine in the front and left side steering.

Several automobile manufacturers started to use governors and float-free carburetors.

# 1901

Two events occurred early in the year that destined the gasoline engine to win out over steam and electric. Near Beaumont, Tex., Spindletop, the fabulous gusher, came in Jan. 10. The price of crude petroleum dropped below five cents a barrel. Nearly two months later

1901—Possibilities of long-distance automobile touring were demonstrated in the New York-to-Buffalo endurance run.

1901 —George N. Pierce in a Pierce Motorette, forerunner of the Pierce-Arrow.

the second event favoring the gasoline engine was a fire that destroyed the Detroit factory of the Olds Motor Works. The only thing saved was an experimental curved-dash roadster. In order to get back in business after the disaster, the firm had no choice but to use that one car as a model and to sub-contract orders for parts and sub-assemblies to small shops in the Detroit area. Most of the operators of these shops thus became automobile manufacturers, and, in conse-quence, Detroit became the Motor City.

The New York-to-Buffalo endurance run demonstrated the possibility of long-distance automobile touring. As a result, automobile Blue Books with route directions were started. The Automobile Club of America launched a pro-

25

gram to place roadside touring signs from New York to Boston.

Connecticut passed laws regulating speed and the registrations of motor vehicles.

The steering wheel had virtually ousted the tiller or lever steering system.

R. E. Olds built 425 curved-dash Oldsmobiles to become the first mass-producer of gasoline automobiles in the world.

David Dunbar Buick, inventor and manufacturer of bathroom appliances, organized Buick Auto-Vim & Power Company, Detroit.

First Jones speedometers used, on Oldsmobiles.

New York State's licenses for motor vehicles added nearly a thousand dollars to the state treasury in the first year.

A total of 88 exhibitors displayed their products at the Second National Automobile Show, Nov. 2–9, in Madison Square Garden. The 1901 show displayed cars that marked the end of the horseless carriage, with the almost universal introduction of the French body type, the tonneau, which was fastened into the car behind the driver's seat and carried two passengers in a pair of seats resembling cut-down barrels.

There was a tendency toward multiple cylinders in the cars exhibited at the show. Water cooling was almost universal among the show cars, and detachable tires became more popular. Improvements were also noted in ignition systems, with the magneto generator coming into more general use.

Roy Dikeman Chapin drove an Oldsmobile from Detroit to New York, covering the distance in 7½ days, at an average of 14 miles per hour.

Electric Vehicle Company, owner of the Selden Patent, threatened suits against automobile manufacturers not licensed by the firm.

A gasoline storage facility for direct service to automobiles became available at an automobile storage and repair station in New York City. The bulk gasoline tank was outside the building as a safety precaution, and connected to the basement by pipe from which gasoline could be dispensed by a self-measuring device, thus eliminating all handling and pouring of the inflammable fluid.

*1902* The popularity of the tonneau body type continued to increase, not only for gasoline cars, but for steam and electric vehicles as well.

The American Automobile Association was organized in Chicago, March 4. The national organization was proposed

1902—The curved-dash Oldsmobile.

four months previously by Frank G. Webb, treasurer of the Long Island Automobile Club.

Thomas B. Jeffery Company introduced the Rambler car and built 1,500 cars during the year.

A 60-day guarantee on new automobiles was adopted by the National Association of Automobile Manufacturers (112 members).

An ordinance was passed in Chicago permitting drivers to wear spectacles, but not *pince-nez* eyeglasses.

Louis S. Clarke, of Autocar Co., designed porcelain spark plug insulation, and patented the double reduction principle in the rear axle construction.

The Motor Mart was established in New York City to buy and sell used cars.

Max Grabowsky organized the Rapid Motor Vehicle Company (in later years it became GMC) to build one-cylinder trucks.

T. H. Shevlin was arrested in Minneapolis for speeding in excess of ten miles an hour and fined $10.

Jonathan Dixon Maxwell joined Charles Brady King to manufacture the Silent Northern, which introduced an integral engine and transmission assembly, three-point suspension of this power unit, and running boards. Maxwell also designed a siphon cooling system which Benjamin and Frank Briscoe manufactured.

Cadillac Automobile Company was formed; the first car was completed Oct. 17.

Oldsmobile production passed the 2,000 mark for the year.

Ohio Automobile Company, successor to the New York and Ohio Co., changed its name to Packard Motor Car Company.

J. Stevens Arms & Tool Company began manufacture of a two-cylinder car called the Stevens-Duryea, designed by J. Frank Duryea.

The Locomobile became the first American gasoline car with a four-cylinder, water-cooled, front-mounted engine.

Electric Vehicle Company was given the right by court decision to make and use Sterling Elliott's steering knuckle. Elliott's principle of steering is still employed on motor vehicles. The principle enables both front wheels to turn instead of the axle, when the steering device is moved.

Packard was granted a patent on Nov. 4 for a gearshift "H" slot, which later became standard for American automobiles.

*1903* Sponsorship of the Third National Automobile Show was shared by the Automobile Club of America and the National Association of Automobile Manufacturers. Cars displayed at the Jan. 17–24 show had several features not seen at the earlier Paris auto show, such as mechanical valves (Rambler and Oldsmobile), compensating carburetors, square "bonnets" and honeycomb radiators. The French style tonneau bodies with a pair of rear seats and closed cars with a "glass front" were feature attractions at the 1903 show.

Cadillac made its first appearance at the 1903 show with a 7.3 horsepower, one-cylinder runabout.

The Ford Motor Company was incorporated with a capitalization of $150,000 in stock; $100,000 issued, and $28,000 paid in cash. Henry Ford, who, as chief engineer of the Detroit Automobile Company, had made several successful racing cars, was named vice president and chief engineer. Original shareholders included John and Horace Dodge, who took stock in exchange for tooling their machine shop to build motors, Albert Strelow, who accepted stock as payment for his carpenter shop which Ford wanted as an assembly plant, Alex Y. Malcolmson, a coal dealer who invested $7,000, Charles J. Woodall and James

1903—The first transcontinental automobile trip was completed by Dr. H. Nelson Jackson and his chauffeur, Sewall K. Crocker, in this two-cylinder Winton from San Francisco to New York City in 63 days.

1903—Barney Oldfield at the tiller of Ford's "999" racer.

Couzens, Malcolmson's employes, John S. Gray, banker and candy manufacturer, John W. Anderson and Horace H. Rackham, attorneys, Vernon Fry, real estate salesman, and Charles H. Bennett, inventor and manufacturer of windmills and air rifles.

The first transcontinental automobile trips were made during the summer of 1903. First to make the long drive was Dr. H. Nelson Jackson of Burlington, Vt., and his chauffeur Sewall K. Crocker. The pair drove a used Winton car, leaving San Francisco on May 23 and arriving in New York on July 26. The second cross-country automobile traveler was Tom Fetch, who, starting June 20, drove a single-cylinder Packard ("Old Pacific") from San Francisco to New York in 53 days. L. L. Whitman and E. T. Hammond made the third San Francisco to New York trip in an Oldsmobile (July 6–Sept. 17).

Packard moved to Detroit, and into the world's first reinforced concrete factory building, designed by Albert Kahn.

The Association of Licensed Automobile Manufacturers was organized. It included the Electric Vehicle Co., the Winton Company, and eight other manufacturers; George H. Day was appointed manager.

The Buick Motor Company was organized with a loan of $1,500 in cash and $2,000 in materials, advanced by Benjamin Briscoe, Jr., and Frank Briscoe. The new firm began making cars with valve-in-head engines.

"MoToR" magazine began its career.

Peerless adopted pressed steel frame construction—one of the major technical improvements during the year.

1903—The Selden Patent Plate. Until 1911, almost every manufacturer of gasoline-propelled vehicles had to pay royalties to holders of this patent through the Association of Licensed Automobile Manufacturers.

1903—Overland, forerunner of the Willys line.

ments during the year. Three other manufacturers used the frame construction shortly afterward.

A power steering arrangement was used in a heavy duty Columbia Electric Motor Truck. A separate electric motor furnished the power.

Ford was sued as an infringer of the Selden patent.

White Steamers made perfect scores in the 650-mile reliability trials held by the Automobile Club of Great Britain and Ireland.

B. A. Gramm perfected a power take-off.

General adoptions this year: T-head cylinders, sliding gear transmissions, mechanically-operated intake valves, and shock absorbers.

Berner Eli ("Barney") Oldfield, former cycle racer, began to achieve fame as the driver of Henry Ford's racer, "999." His chief competitors were Wridgeway, in a Peerless, Fosdick, in a Winton, Carl Fisher, in a Mohawk, Walter C.

Baker, in the "Torpedo Kid," and Charles Schmidt, in a Packard.

The Brownlow-Latimer Federal Good Roads Bill, first of its kind to be introduced in Congress, received strong support from the automotive industry and automobile clubs across the nation. The bill died in committee.

*1904* The Fourth National Automobile Show, held Jan. 16–23, was larger than any of its predecessors, with 185 exhibitors, including 87 automobile exhibits. A "convertible" of sorts made its appearance at this show: a touring car, to which could be attached a glass-sided, solid top, called "California top" for use in inclement weather.

Automatic lubrication was another feature found on some cars, including the Autocar. Some models featured a fan to cool the water pipes used in the engine cooling system. Standard quick-demountable rims appeared on many new cars.

Studebaker sold its first gasoline motor vehicle.

R. E. Olds sold his interest in the Olds Motor Works, and organized the Reo Motor Car Company.

The Detroit Y.M.C.A. established a school for automobile mechanics.

Carl Graham Fisher and James A. Allison organized the Prest-O-Lite Company to perfect a safe method of using acetylene gas for automobile headlights.

Leland & Faulconer Manufacturing Company was merged with Cadillac Automobile Company and the name was changed to the Cadillac Motor Car Company.

The first White bus appeared.

A disastrous fire at the Cadillac plant delayed production and forced the company to return dealer deposits on 1,500 cars.

1904—Electric cars were popular among women.

1904—A 1,258 mile motor tour from New York to St. Louis was the forerunner of the famous Glidden Tours.

1904—A test run conducted by an express company showed motor trucks made more deliveries in better time, went farther and occupied less ground space than horses.

1904—The First Vander-
bilt Cup Race was held on
Long Island.

Pope-Hartford was criticized by competitors for including lamps as standard equipment.

The Fischer car was equipped with an air brake system for the rear wheels and drive sprockets. An auxiliary engine powered the air compressor.

The National Association of Retail Automobile Dealers was formed.

Ford Motor Company opened its first branch (on Jefferson Avenue, Detroit).

One of the earliest cars in the U. S. to attempt an automatic transmission was the Sturtevant. The car featured a centrifugal clutch which had low and high speed ranges. The Sturtevant also featured an air brake system.

A motor tour of 1,258 miles was organized to drive from New York to the Louisiana Purchase Exposition in St. Louis. Of the 71 cars that started, only 59 reached St. Louis. Col. Augustus Post, general chairman of the pilgrimage, gave the signal to start the 17-day motor trip on July 25. One of the tourists, Charles Glidden, impressed with the tour, later proposed what became the famous Glidden Tours.

The first Vanderbilt Cup Race was held Oct. 8 on Long Island.

# 1905

The trend toward large gasoline cars was noticeable at the Fifth National Automobile Show at Madison Square Garden—177 were gasoline cars, 4 steam cars and 31 electrics, including 9 electric trucks. Only one car (Waltham Buckboard) had wire spokes—all others had artillery type wheels with wood or steel spokes) The French tonneau with a rear door had been replaced by longer bodies with side doors. Comfort and ease in riding were stressed in the new models; speed was secondary.

1905—Motor ca provided new mo bility, brought the country close tc city folks.

1905—Two Olds mobiles, "Olc Scout" and "Olc Steady," com pleted a transcon tinental race fron New York to Port land in 44 days.

1905—Lined up in front of the Mt. Washington Hotel in New Hampshire are 36 of the cars, including four non-contestants, in the first Glidden Tour. The tour covered 870 miles from New York City to Bretton Woods, N. H. and return.

Cape or folding tops were introduced by several manufacturers, and some replaced the canopy tops.

The first Glidden tour of 870 miles was routed from New York to the White Mountains and return. Percy Pierce with a Pierce-Arrow won the award.

The Society of Automobile Engineers was formed.

Cars were sold on the installment plan.

The American Motor Car Manufacturers Association was organized.

Two Oldsmobiles completed a transcontinental race from New York to Portland, Oregon, in 44 days.

The Ariel car offered a motor air cooled in winter and water cooled in summer.

Bus operations were started on New York's First Avenue.

The Holsman Motor Buggy offered 48-inch wheels; the Stearns boasted a 119-inch wheelbase.

A bill was introduced in the 59th Congress to regulate the operation of automobiles and other motor vehicles by the states. This, the first attempt by the Federal government to regulate motor vehicles, died in committee.

The Diamond T Company was organized by C. A. Tilt.

Motor trucks were introduced by many automobile makers, including Packard, Oldsmobile, Maxwell, and Mitchell.

Innovations during the year included: Gabriel exhaust horn, Weed tire chains, Goodyear universal rims to take either clincher or straight side tires, power tire pump, and ignition lock.

*1906* Cars displayed at the Sixth National Automobile Show indicated that manufacturers were striving to develop better and stronger materials—chrome-nickel steel, phosphor bronze and high carbon steel were prominent. The Marmon cast aluminum body was an example of attempts to build lighter cars.

A Stanley Steamer, with Fred Marriott driving, ran a mile in 28⅕ seconds, averaging 127.66 m.p.h., at Ormond Beach, Fla., Jan. 27.

Buick included a storage battery as standard equipment.

Six-cylinder cars were the talk of the country. National, Stevens-Duryea, Ford, Franklin and Pierce-Arrow offered six's.

Motor vehicles aided in relief operations following the San Francisco earthquake and fire. Walter C. White organized a caravan of White trucks in Los Angeles to carry help and supplies to the victims of the stricken city.

Prest-O tire tanks were introduced for tire inflation; each

1906—Fred Marriott became the first human to travel more than two miles a minute when the streamlined Stanley Steamer "Rocket" averaged 127.66 mph at Ormond-Daytona Beach on Jan. 27.

tank had the capacity to inflate 25 tires of 34 × 4 size up to 80 pounds pressure.

In addition to the craze for six-cylinder cars, a wide variety of engines was offered by some manufacturers.

Reo had its first four-cylinder car; Olds introduced a two-cycle engine; Maxwell built a 12-cylinder racer; and Adams-Farwell offered three- and five-cylinder rotary engines, an innovation which later influenced rotary aviation engines.

Front bumpers appeared on some cars, but not as standard equipment.

L. L. Whitman drove a Franklin from New York to San Francisco in 15 days, 2 hours, 15 minutes.

Backed by Edwin Ross Thomas, Buffalo manufacturer, Roy D. Chapin, Howard E. Coffin, Frederick O. Bezner

1906—Motor vehicles were used extensively in relief and rescue operations following the earthquake and fire that destroyed much of San Francisco.

1906—The date "1877" on the car repre sents the year in which the invention wa conceived. Patent Office rules permitted th inventor to assert a date of invention tw years prior to the date of his patent applica tion—in Selden's case, 1879.

and James J. Brady, former Olds employees, organized the E. R. Thomas-Detroit Company.

Automobile plants in Detroit produced 550 to 600 cars a week. Packard alone built an average of six cars a day.

## 1907 Technical advances noted by the press at the Seventh National Automobile Show, Jan. 12–19, were the prevalence of selective transmissions, a gain in six-cylinder engines, larger brakes (some equipped with

1907—An air-cooled Franklin light runabout crosses a stream that flows over an early road.

camel's hair cloth covering on the friction surfaces—fore-runner of modern asbestos brake lining), improved body finishes (up to 30 coats of paint), and twin carburetors (on the Stearns, Columbia and Matheson).

The first motor truck show was staged in Chicago.

International Harvester Company built its first automotive vehicle in January, 1907, in Chicago. The truck plant then was moved to Akron, Ohio, in October, 1907.

Oakland Motor Car Company was organized by Edward M. Murphy, buggy builder, of Pontiac, Mich., to make a two-cylinder car designed by Alanson P. Brush. Nineteen

1907—Maxwell, along with other manufacturers, designed cars especially for doctors. This is the "Doctor Model."

1907—One of the first International motor trucks was an "Auto Wagon" produced in 1907. All models through 1915 were right-hand drive.

years later Oakland introduced a companion car, the Pontiac, which survived the parent.

Gasoline economy runs were much in vogue; one of the most popular was conducted in Chicago.

Henry Ford purchased 60 acres of land in Highland Park, Mich., and started construction of a new factory.

Hewitt introduced a V-8 limousine, the first U. S. production touring car with an eight-cylinder engine.

A Reo crossed and re-crossed the continent, negotiating such climbs as Mt. Hood and Raton Range.

The Association of Licensed Automobile Manufacturers presented a formula for figuring horsepower; the formula was adopted by many states as a basis for taxation.

Oldsmobile employed nickel plating for trim parts that had hitherto been brass.

Humps were purposely built into streets at Glencoe, Ill., to discourage speeding.

Buick adopted a four-cylinder engine with a sliding-gear transmission, and won the Dead Horse Hill Climb at Worcester, Mass.

A Franklin was driven 1,060 miles from New York to Chicago in 39 hours, 36 minutes.

A bill was introduced in Congress providing for regulation of speed, identification and registration of motor vehicles engaged in interstate travel. Supported by motor vehicle manufacturers and automobile clubs, it died before it reached the floor of the House of Representatives.

Engine timing gears were enclosed in many cars. Mud aprons were becoming more general under the engine.

Autocar introduced a truck with a shaft-driven axle.

Despite the business depression, both Packard and Ford made profits of more than a million dollars.

*1908* Wheelbases on most of the new models were longer, and manufacturers moved the rear seats toward the center of the car to provide more comfort. The four-cylinder vertical engine was almost standard at the Eighth National Automobile Show. Most of the cars exhibited offered sliding gear transmissions. Other mechanical improvements included the increased accessibility of parts, bigger and better brakes, better enclosed clutches, and easier controls.

General Motors Company was incorporated in New Jersey by William Crapo Durant, with William Eaton as first president.

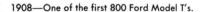

1908—One of the first 800 Ford Model T's.

1908—The famous Thomas Flyer, winner of the New York to Paris race.

Cadillac became the first American car manufacturer to win the Dewar Trophy, awarded by the Royal Automobile Club of Great Britain for the greatest contribution to advancement of the industry. Cadillac was honored for interchangeability of parts.

The Model T Ford made its first appearance on Oct. 1.

1908—A Thomas taxi cab in Central Park. The meter was an innovation.

A four-cylinder, 60-horsepower Thomas Flyer won the New York-to-Paris Race, which began in Times Square on Feb. 12, headed westward, and ended 170 days later in Paris. The Thomas car drove a total of 13,341 miles in 88 days with an average of 151 miles per day.

J. M. Murdock of Johnstown, Pa., was the first motorist to drive his family across the U. S. They left Los Angeles on April 24 and arrived in New York on May 26.

The Columbia Mark XLVI used a gasoline engine to drive an electric generator. From this generator, separate electric motors propelled the wheels. The aim of this "gasolect" car was to provide a smooth flow of power by eliminating the conventional gear shift transmission.

Buick, Oldsmobile and Oakland became units of General Motors.

C. Harold Wills developed the use of vanadium steel for Ford.

Pierce-Arrow won fourth successive victory in the fourth Glidden Tour.

John North Willys was made president and general manager of Overland, which became Willys-Overland.

Fred J. and Charles T. Fisher organized Fisher Body Company.

Rapid Motor Vehicle Company (trucks) became part of General Motors.

Autocar discontinued passenger car production to concentrate on 1½ ton trucks of 97 in. wheelbase, with engines under the seat.

Otto Zachow and William Besserdich, of Clintonville, Wis. developed the first successful four-wheel drive motor vehicle.

Innovations: Stewart magnetic speedometers; Charles Y. Knight's invention of sleeve-valve engines; left-hand steering; silent timing chains; motor-driven horns; baked enamel finishes; helical gears.

The Commercial Car Manufacturers Association was formed, with G. M. Weeks as president and Walter Wardrop as manager.

# 1909

At the Ninth National Automobile Show, more emphasis was placed on pleasing the public than on booking orders from dealers. Four-cylinder cars ac-

1909—Mrs. John R. Ramsey and three companions in a Maxwell touring car were the first women to drive an automobile across the U. S.

counted for 71 per cent of the gasoline automobiles, 27 per cent were six-cylinder, and only two single-cylinder models were displayed. Air self-starters were found on several of the cars exhibited. Another new feature was a steering wheel with the under side corrugated so the driver's hand would not slip.

First rural mile of concrete pavement in the U. S. opened July 4 in Wayne County, Mich. The pavement was constructed on Woodward Avenue (now U. S. 10) between Six Mile and Seven Mile Roads, at a cost of $13,534.59.

Louis Chevrolet, famous racer, began work on a six-cylinder passenger car of his own design in his Detroit shop.

The Selden Patent was sustained as valid and infringed upon by Ford.

Mrs. John R. Ramsey became the first woman to drive across the U. S. She left New York in a Maxwell car with three women companions on June 9, and arrived in San Francisco 53 days later.

W. S. Seaman & Company (later Seaman Body Corp.) built the first automobile bodies in Milwaukee.

Carl Graham Fisher and his associates completed the first Indianapolis Speedway. After the first races on Aug. 19, the track was paved with brick for a two-day meet in December.

The Hudson Motor Car Company was organized.

Cadillac was one of many companies that became part of General Motors during 1909. General Motors paid its first preferred stock dividend.

Gramm trucks featured overdrive transmissions.

The White Company built a gasoline engine car to replace the famous White Steamer.

The 1909 Glidden Tour from Detroit to Denver and back to Kansas City covered 2,636 miles—the longest Glidden Tour up to that time.

Fabric tops, often called "one-man tops," appeared on the market.

The year was marked by an acceleration of earlier trends in engineering, production techniques and uses of materials: magnetos showed a steady gain; cellular radiators were gradually displacing tubular ones; high-tension ignition systems were used on the majority of cars instead of the make-and-break system; selective gearsets had a 10-to-1 lead over the progressive type. The fashion was to cast cylinders in pairs, but the block casting was getting under way in small models; and there was a large increase in the use of chrome nickel steel and vanadium steel.

At the end of the year there were 290 different makes of automobiles produced at 145 cities in 24 states. Detroit had 25 different car makes and a total of 45 makes were produced in Michigan. Chicago had the second highest number with 14 different brands, then Indianapolis with 12 and Cleveland with 10. Indiana rated second among states with 44 and Ohio third with 39 makes.

*1910* A new type of automobile body made its first appearance in the U. S. at the 10th National Automobile Show, the *torpedo*. This new body resembled a bathtub on wheels. The dashboard and its instruments were brought up closer to the driver, by means of a cowl, and the sides were extended upward, in some cases almost to shoulder height. Previously, motorists and their passengers had perched on cars, high and exposed; now they could sit in them, low and sheltered.

The year witnessed a trend toward standardization: many car makers changing transmission, motor starting or some other detail to bring their cars in line with the rest of the field. Clutches, however, still showed great variety—and little efficiency. Haynes used a contracting band; E-M-F had a leather-faced cone with cork insert; Rambler used the Borg & Beck single plate clutch; and Knox, Thomas and Stevens Duryea featured a multiple-disc clutch.

Several important marketing changes took place. The Owen car, designed by Ralph Owen, offered as standard equipment: top, windshield, electric horn, electric-acetylene headlamps, electric-oil side lamps and an electric tail lamp.

1910—The Owen offered a top, windshield, electric horn, headlamps and a tail lamp as standard equipment.

1910—Motorists had their problems—poor roads, flat tires and almost no protection from the weather.

Another make, the Overland, announced its model "38" as a completely equipped car at $1,000 and was the first car in this class to carry as standard equipment at list price a top, windshield, lamps and magneto.

Benjamin Briscoe started the $16,000,000 United States Motor Car Corporation by combining and affiliating 130 separate companies with the firm. Some of these included Columbia Motor Car Company (successor to the Electric Vehicle Company that controlled the Selden patent), Brush Runabout Company, Alden Sampson Company, Dayton Motor Car Company and Maxwell-Briscoe Motor Company. (Over-expansion and lack of working capital forced United States Motor Car Company into receivership in September, 1912.)

Major Henry Souther headed the first Standardization Committee of the Society of Automobile Engineers after having directed standardization of parts as an activity of the A.L.A.M.

Reo announced its Speed Wagon, a low-priced light delivery truck.

Four Wheel Drive Auto Company, Clintonville, Wis., began manufacture of four-wheel drive vehicles.

Racing at Indianapolis Speedway this year featured a three-day series ending May 31, a three-day meet ending July 4, and two days of racing on Sept. 3 and 4.

American LaFrance Fire Engine Company, a fire engine manufacturer for 75 years, produced its first fire-fighting motor vehicle.

Automobile production started at the Ford Motor Company, Highland Park plant.

G. A. Schacht produced a complete line of trucks, from a 1,000-pound delivery unit to a three-ton chain-drive chassis.

Patents were issued on the Knight valve principle which was the forerunner of the Knight engine to be introduced in the U. S. in 1911.

Central Oil Co. built what may have been the first drive-in gasoline station with an island, in Detroit.

1911—The first transcontinental motor truck trip was made by a Saurer truck.

# 1911

The four-door car became popular at the 1911 National Automobile Show—nearly every manufacturer exhibited a model.

The first truck show in Madison Square Garden was held during the second week of the 11th National Automobile Show. The commercial phase of the show had 286 exhibitors, including 27 gasoline vehicles, 7 electric displays, and 18 motorcycle stands.

The hazards of starting engines by hand-cranking were reflected in the devices offered during the year as hopeful solutions of the problem. An Amplex had a compressed-air starter; also available for nearly all cars was the Geiszler Starting Device, an apparatus that was supposed to start the engine with an electric charge.

The Selden Patent, previously sustained in the U. S. District Court, was declared "valid but not infringed" by Ford and other manufacturers, in the U. S. Court of Appeals. (The payment of royalties that disrupted the early industry had come to an end.)

The first transcontinental motor-truck trip was made by a Saurer truck. The tour started on March 4 from Denver to Los Angeles and then to San Francisco. The truck was

1911—A Mack fire truck equipped with the first Gould pump.

then shipped by railroad back to Pueblo, Colorado, where the eastward leg of the journey began on June 12 under its own power for New York.

Pierce-Arrow added a five-ton truck to its line of passenger cars.

Diamond T Motor Car Company discontinued making passenger cars to concentrate on trucks.

General Motors Truck Company was formed by combining the Rapid and Reliance Truck Companies.

Hudson offered a "simplified chassis" (including a new four-cylinder block engine with cross-shaft in front carrying magneto and water pump) and multiple disc clutch.

International Motor Company (Mack) was formed by consolidation of Mack Bros. Motor Car Co., Saurer Motor Company, and Hewitt Motor Company.

Edward N. Hines originated painted center lines on highways in Wayne County (Detroit), Mich.

Chevrolet Motor Company of Michigan was organized in November, and production began.

The first 500-mile Indianapolis Speedway Race was won by Ray Harroun in a six-cylinder Marmon "Wasp," which introduced the first use of a rearview mirror in the U.S. Time: 6 hours, 42 minutes, 8 seconds.

For the first time, securities of automotive companies were listed on the New York Stock Exchange.

The Studebaker Corporation was formed, and manufacture of electric vehicles was discontinued to allow concentration on gasoline cars.

Knight sleeve-valve engines were introduced on the American market by Stearns, Stoddard-Dayton, and Columbia.

## 1912
The 12th National Automobile Show was sponsored by the new Automobile Board of Trade, formed to succeed the A.L.A.M. which disbanded in 1911.

1912—First Brockway truck.

The self-starter was the vogue at the 1912 show. There were 13 types of acetylene starters on display, 6 compressed air, 7 electric, 14 mechanical, 2 gasoline and 1—the Winton— exhaust gas.

At the commercial display, during the second week of the National Automobile Show, a five-ton Sampson coal truck was equipped with a compressed air device for dumping. Pope-Hartford's new truck, the first built by the company, had a tilting cab for access to the motor located under the seat. The new General Motors Trucks were exhibited for the first time.

Steward Motor Corporation was formed to make cars and trucks.

A Packard truck was the first truck to cross the continent from the East Coast to the Pacific Coast. It carried a three-ton load from New York to San Francisco in 46 days.

Cadillac adopted an electric starter developed by Charles F. Kettering of the Dayton Engineering Laboratories Company (Delco), along with a generator-battery lighting system.

The all-steel body developed by Edward Gowen Budd (an open car model), was offered by Oakland and Hupmobile.

Engine temperature indicator, the Boyce Moto-Meter, was introduced.

Chicago adopted an ordinance limiting horn use.

Electric car makers organized and held separate shows.

George A. Brockway, famous carriage-builder, organized the Brockway Motor Company to build trucks.

Philadelphia held a commercial wagon parade in which 500 trucks participated.

*1913* A single ticket at the 13th National Automobile Show was good for the double showings in both Madison Square Garden and Grand Central Palace. The

1913—The Model T's popularity led the way to mass production. This overhead body drop at the Ford Highland Park (Mich.) plant was one of the features which speeded output.

popular priced cars were on display at the Palace and the high-priced and high-powered cars were at the Garden. A general trend toward sloping fronts and hoods was noticed at the 1913 show, along with strides toward smoother lines and longer curves. Designers went back to colonial days and Louis XIV coaches for the popular coupes, which flared out at the top.

Dealers, worried about used car sales, asked the National Association of Automobile Manufacturers to investigate.

The National Automobile Chamber of Commerce was organized (predecessor of the Automobile Manufacturers Association, Inc.) through a merger of the Automobile Board of Trade and the National Association of Automobile Manufacturers.

A standard 90-day warranty for passenger cars and commercial vehicles was recommended to its members by the NACC.

Chevrolet operations were moved to Flint and merged with the Little Motor Car Company.

Installment paper was used in automobile financing.

Cadillac won the Dewar Trophy for the second time. The award was given for the development of the electric starter.

Wire wheels were offered as standard equipment on several production cars.

The Bendix drive for electric starters was shown for the first time.

Ford production attained a rate of a thousand cars a day.

Kissel Kar introduced a new wrap-around windshield on several of its 1913 models, though it wasn't called by that name.

The National Association of Automobile Advertising Men was organized.

Packard used forced feed lubrication and worm bevel gears.

The first Chevrolet assembly plant was opened.

The Thomas B. Jeffery Company introduced the four-wheel-drive Quad truck.

Carl Graham Fisher, who was promoting an ocean-to-ocean highway, turned his pledges over to the Lincoln Highway Association.

Pierce-Arrow put headlamps on the mudguards.

Spaulding touring cars were equipped with folding backs on front seats in order to convert into beds. Electric reading lamps and air mattresses were included.

Gulf Oil Company was the first U. S. petroleum firm to distribute free road maps.

## 1914 The 14th National Automobile Show at Grand Central Palace in New York City was sponsored by the newly formed National Automobile Chamber of Commerce.

1914—First stop sign used to control traffic was in Detroit.

57

A novelty of the 1914 show was the display of cyclecars. There were five such showings of these tiny one- and two-passenger vehicles. One cyclecar, the Argo, was priced at $295. The first cyclecars had appeared in 1913, and had been dismissed as "toys" and "a silly fad" by most motorists and vehicle manufacturers. After their formal debut at the National Automobile Show, the market for them expanded enormously. The craze was, however, short-lived; few of the little "economy" vehicles remained on the market after 1915.

During the show week Henry Ford announced a $5 minimum daily wage (including a profit-sharing plan) for all non-salary employees over 22 years of age, and an eight-hour day.

Chevrolet discontinued its six-cylinder model, and began making four-cylinder cars.

Cadillac developed and introduced a V-8 high-speed automobile engine.

The Rambler's name was changed to Jeffery.

Horace and John Dodge started production of the Dodge automobile.

Alfred Reeves became general manager of the National Automobile Chamber of Commerce.

Hand brake at driver's left was introduced by Packard.

Maxwell offered an adjustable driver's seat.

A Detroit ordinance prohibited gasoline pumps at curbs.

The first stop sign to control traffic was installed in Detroit.

Electric traffic lights were installed in Cleveland, Ohio, in August.

Henry Ford announced plans to rebate between $40 to $60 to each purchaser of a new Ford Model T providing the Ford Motor Company sold more than 300,000 cars from August, 1914, to August, 1915.

The traffic department of the National Automobile

Chamber of Commerce suggested dimensions of automobile box cars to railroad companies. The NACC also drafted a road-building code, setting forth the views of the automobile manufacturers on highway conditions.

The Society of Automobile Engineers organized several research committees to study gas-electric vehicles, kerosene carburetors, greases, engine characteristics, governors, and non-electric continuous torque transmission.

Buick changed to a six-cylinder engine.

*1915* The outstanding feature of the 1915 National Automobile Show was the eight-cylinder engine. Cadillac, King, Briggs-Detroiter and Remington all offered such engines. Cadillac introduced a V-8 several months before.

Another auto show attraction was the "sociable" body offered by Packard, Winton, Kline and Kissell, with the corridor or salon body with an aisle between the two front seats allowing passengers to move freely between front and back seats. Another novel car was the Gadabout roadster with a wicker body. The National had another original seating arrangement—four armchairs that could be moved on casters in any direction.

There were no cyclecars exhibited at the 1915 show, thus signaling the end of the short-lived fad.

Briscoe and Owen offered convertible roadsters on which the top, when down, was completely concealed at the rear of the body.

Packard added a 12-cylinder model, the "Twin Six," America's first, and the first automobile engine with aluminum pistons.

Franklin put the spare tire in the trunk of its roadster model.

Ford production passed one million cars.

1915—This Saxon, priced $395, illustrates the trend to light cars in this period.

General Motors declared its first dividend ($50 a share) on common stock.

The Liberty Bell was transported from Philadelphia to the Panama-Pacific Exposition by a White Truck.

A solid metal wheel was offered on the Jeffery truck.

Demountable rims replaced the clincher types.

Cadillac offered tilt-beam headlamps.

Oldsmobile offered a top and windshield as standard equipment.

World War I began to create material shortages.

During this year a great wave of five-cent jitneys arose in various cities that had been hit by transit strikes.

Automobiles were admitted to Yellowstone National Park on Aug. 1 over a carefully prepared one-way route.

Truck production began to assume importance as the war in Europe demonstrated the worth of motor trucks.

Ford Motor Company refunded $50 to those who purchased Model T's between August, 1914 and August, 1915. Checks were distributed Aug. 15.

Prism lenses for headlights made their first appearance.

There were approximately 450 automotive and auto parts manufacturers in the U. S. by the end of 1915.

*1916* New models displayed at the 16th National Automobile Show generally featured lower prices and more powerful engines. Most of the cars were under $1,250, including many six-cylinder models. Five manufacturers— Enger, Haynes, National, Packard and Pathfinder—exhibited 12-cylinder models.

New design features noted at the 1916 show included the slanted windshields, and double-cowl bodies, in which

1915—The Briscoe featured a "cyclops-eye" headlight.

"tonneau cowls" separated front and back seats. Increased use of wire wheels was also noted.

Studebaker displayed a gold chassis reportedly worth $25,000 at the 1916 National Automobile Show. The most unusual car exhibited, however, was the light-weight Marmon 34, with aluminum body and fenders, aluminum engine castings and other aluminum parts. The seven-passenger touring car, with a wheelbase of 136 inches, weighed only 3,540 pounds.

Charles W. Nash left General Motors to take over the Thomas B. Jeffery Company and form Nash Motors Company.

A General Motors one-ton truck established a record for an endurance run by hauling a load of canned milk from Seattle to New York in 30 days.

The number of makes offering V-8 engines grew to 18

1916—Passage of the Federal Road Aid Act was the beginning of a nation-wide system of interstate highways.

models. They included: Abbott, Apperson, Briscoe, Cadillac, Cole, Daniels, Hollier, Jackson, King, Monarch, Oakland, Oldsmobile, Peerless, Pilot, Ross, Scripps-Booth, Standard and Stearns-Knight.

The Fordson Tractor was announced by Ford Motor Company.

Ford bought a factory site on the banks of the Rouge River in Dearborn, Mich.

The U. S. Army used a fleet of trucks as a supply train for an expeditionary force in Mexico.

The National Automobile Chamber of Commerce passed a resolution branding the advertisement of deferred payments as "unethical."

United Motors Corporation was formed with Alfred P. Sloan, Jr., as president.

Hand-operated windshield wipers, stop lights, and rear-view mirrors appeared as standard equipment on several cars.

Cross licensing agreements pertaining to patents became effective in the auto industry.

Prices of gasoline and automobiles advanced during the year, and economy tests of stock cars became so numerous that the Society of Automobile Engineers published requirements for such tests if they were to be recognized.

The Federal Aid Road Act, signed by President Woodrow Wilson on July 11, was the first Federal law aimed at the establishment of a nation-wide system of interstate highways. The act provided for the construction of "rural public roads" and defined them as "any public road over which the United States mails now are or may hereafter be transported." Federal contributions would not exceed 50 per cent of the total cost of each project, and the matching portion would be furnished by the states. The act also puts more emphasis upon the organization of a state highway department before a state could receive Federal highway aid.

1917—The first Nash-designed car had a six-cylinder valve-in-head engine.

*1917* All car and truck manufacturers offered full co-operation to the government as the United States entered World War I.

Many automotive companies participated in the development and production of Liberty aircraft engines, designed by Jesse G. Vincent and E. J. Hall.

The first Nash appeared, with a six-cylinder valve-in-head engine.

Henry M. Leland, former president of Cadillac, formed the Lincoln Motor Company.

Chevrolet offered a V-8 model.

Studebaker developed and adopted an internal manifold hot-spot to vaporize the fuel mixture more efficiently.

The Society of Automobile Engineers became the Society of Automotive Engineers (S.A.E.).

Paige introduced a coupe with a rumble seat and a V-type windshield.

Hudson Motor Car Company organized the Essex Motor Car Company to manufacture a light car.

64

Several closed cars exhibited at the 1917 National Automobile Show were equipped with heaters.

Frederick Furber developed a built-in radiator shutter which was introduced by Columbia.

John North Willys and Col. Charles Clifton represented the automotive industry on the National Industrial Conference Board.

The largest truck contract was announced between Kelly-Springfield Co., and the United States Circus Corp., for 100 trucks. The circus planned to use the 3½-ton trucks instead of rail cars for transporting the tent show.

By the end of the year various boards for organizing the motor industry were formed to bring about the standardization of design for war production. The result of large war contracts was seen in a considerable number of mergers and an extraordinary number of capital stock increases.

*1918* The country was in the midst of war when the 18th National Automobile Show was held at New York's Grand Central Palace. There were fuel shortages of coal and petroleum, due mainly to the nation's almost total dependence for transportation, on war-burdened railroads, and talk of the possibility that motor vehicle production would be curtailed, or even stopped altogether. As far as official Washington was concerned, motor vehicles were dispensable luxuries, and the wartime excise levies taxed them as if they were tobacco, whiskey, furs, perfume or jewelry.

Factories were turned over to war work, men drafted into the army, and women took their places at benches, machine tools, and even in repair shops. The industry's war production included shells, helmets, caissons, aircraft engines, tractors, tanks, naval craft, anti-aircraft guns, gun carriages, artillery recoil mechanisms, in addition to military vehicles.

1918—Motor trucks proved their value in the first World War. Typical are these White two-ton models shown in convoy in France.

Because of the war, accessory and automobile manufacturers offered many new devices for prolonging the life of cars, and introduced carburetors designed to use low-grade fuels and even kerosene.

There were heatless days and gasless Sundays to conserve fuel; everything was done to check the use of motor cars unless vehicle travel was necessary. Motorless Sundays ended Oct. 13.

Designers borrowed from the armored cars and other military vehicles that were produced at the time. Four cars—Paige, Oldsmobile, McFarlan and Anderson—had steel wheels that resembled military wheels. Straight lines, higher hoods and the steel wheels gave many of the new models a war-like appearance.

Closed cars (which were 10 per cent of production) had more glass area in 1918, giving more visibility. More attention was given to the driver's seat of closed cars for those owners who wanted to do their own driving, their chauffeurs having become part of the war effort.

The first unit of highway construction authorized under the Federal Aid Road Act of 1916 was completed Jan. 30, from Richmond to the Alameda County line in California. The 2.55 mile road was built at a cost of $53,938.85, of which Federal aid totaled $24,244.56.

Four-wheel hydraulic brakes were developed by Malcolm Loughead of California. Along with E. A. Featherstone, D. O. Scott and Otto C. Lang, Loughead (Lockheed) formed a company to promote the patents which were used later (in 1920) on production automobiles.

Passenger car production, already curtailed by plant facility shortages, was given a government steel allocation to balance their inventories for building 50 per cent of the cars produced during the previous year. After the armistice in November, the percentage was increased to 75 per cent.

White discontinued passenger car production to concentrate on trucks.

Chevrolet became part of General Motors.

Nash became the world's largest producer of trucks this year with an Army contract for 11,494 units.

The National Automobile Dealers Association was organized in Washington in response to a call from F.W.A. Vesper to combat a threat to take all men out of the dealer shops.

As the year closed, the price situation puzzled all car makers. The fact was that cheaper materials were expected, but prices did not drop. The troubles of readjustment were at hand.

1919—Essex helped boost the popularity of the economical closed car.

*1919* Few new ideas were exhibited at the 19th National Automobile Show; there was too little time after the armistice to work on new models. Some manufacturers, however, did bring out changes in design and detail, particularly better brakes, wiring, and suspension. The war had taught ways of improving these three parts. A low-priced, four cylinder Essex, made by Hudson, was the only new car at the Show. A white Daniels sport touring car displayed a golf bag attachment over the running board for the eager golfer who liked to be ready when he passed a country club.

The flat rate system of repair was tried out.

Ford produced 750,000 cars, more than one-third of the industry's total output.

1919—A Hupmobile touring car at Yosemite Falls, Calif.

General Motors Acceptance Corporation was formed.

Studebaker discontinued carriage making to concentrate on motor vehicles.

G. A. Schacht perfected a "two-range" truck transmission featuring eight forward speeds and two reverse speeds.

Henry Ford bought out minority stockholders, and Edsel Bryant Ford became president of Ford Motor Company.

Front and rear bumpers were offered as standard equipment on the Westcott touring car.

Having built and sold 30,000 small trucks since 1908, Autocar adopted a short wheelbase and engine-under-seat design for 2- and 5-ton trucks.

The world's first three-color traffic control light was installed in Detroit, and Detroit police pioneered in offering safety instruction in school classrooms.

Car makers were swamped with orders by May, but were unable to fill them because of parts and material shortages.

Strikes, rising wages, and a shortage of automobiles were major problems confronting the automotive industry in July as dealers were clamoring for new models.

General Motors bought an interest in Fisher Body Company, and Nash bought an interest in the Seaman Body Corporation.

Indirect lighting of instruments on the dash appeared on

some cars. Approximately 90 per cent of all passenger cars made during the year were open models, i.e., touring cars and roadsters.

*1920* The first post-war National Automobile Show sponsored by the National Automobile Chamber of Commerce was held Jan. 3 through Jan. 10. Closed cars continued to gain over open cars (119 closed models in 1920 compared with 79 in the previous show). The marked change in the cars displayed was the increase in the number of owner-driven, as opposed to chauffeur-driven cars. Convertible cars had almost disappeared—only two were displayed at the show. (At that time, the term "convertible" meant a touring car or roadster which could be purchased, for about $500, a "California top"—a solid-roofed structure with glazed windows—which could be stored in a stable or garage in summer, but would replace the folding fabric top in autumn.)

Sloping windshields were evident everywhere. Also, heaters were standard equipment. Wire wheels were more numerous than wooden artillery wheels.

Buick and McFarlan offered solid metal wheels on passenger cars.

A compass and camera were offered as standard equipment on the Templar touring roadster. Flower vases were part of the standard equipment on the sedan model.

General Motors Research Corporation was organized under the direction of C. F. Kettering.

Duesenberg appeared; it was the first U. S. car with a straight-eight engine and first licensee to use hydraulic four-wheel brakes developed by Malcolm Loughead in 1918.

Packard introduced the Lanchester vibration dampener.

William C. Durant again lost control of General Motors, and Pierre S. duPont was named president.

1920—Bullet-shaped headlamps were one of the features on the Kissel. The hood ventilator cooled the engine in the summer and permitted fumes to escape.

1920—Dort touring car.

In May the manager of the Kansas City Federal Reserve Bank declined to discount any paper from member banks based on passenger car stocks. This action caused great concern within the automotive industry, for it meant a tightening of credit.

A railroad strike curtailed transportation of freight. The motor truck proved its qualities by carrying great loads of long and short haul freight. Freight embargoes also promoted driveaways and river shipments of automobiles.

In August, a bankers' committee took over the Maxwell plant.

A nation-wide program of highway research on a large scale was launched. As a result of problems in highway construction and maintenance, the Highway Research Board of the National Research Council was organized. Tests on experimental roads were conducted at Arlington, Va., Pittsburg, Calif., and near Springfield, Ill.

By October, completion of Federal-aid highway projects totaled 191 miles.

Mack had rubber engine mountings and rubber spring shackles.

*1921* Most popular body type at the 21st National Automobile Show was the open touring car, seating five, six, or seven passengers. Glass windshield wings made their eastern debut—the first seen at a New York show, although they had been popular for years in Southern California.

The post-war depression brought a drastic curtailment of sales.

Studebaker developed nickel-molybdenum steel for commercial use.

Ford weathered a financial crisis with the help of dealers. Ford car production passed the five million mark, or 55.45 per cent of the industry's total output.

Hudson offered a coach, the Essex, priced at only $300 more than a touring car.

Fred M. Zeder, Owen R. Skelton and Carl Breer incorporated as consulting automotive engineers to begin design of cars with new concepts. Later the Chrysler was one of their cars.

W. C. Durant retired from General Motors directorate and organized Durant Motors, Inc.

Nickel plating appeared on radiators and lamps.

Cadillac offered thermostatic control of carburetion.

On March 4, Warren G. Harding became the first U. S. President to ride in an automobile to his inauguration. The car was a Packard Twin-Six.

1921—A distinctive feature of the Willys-Knight was the sleeve-valve engine that reportedly "improved with use."

1921—The famous Stutz Bearcat.

Cadillac moved into a new factory on Clark Avenue, Detroit, Mich.

Detroit police experimented with synchronized traffic signal lights, and raised-platform safety zones.

The General Motors Building in Detroit was opened, and became the home of many departments of the corporation.

Herbert Hoover, Secretary of Commerce, asked the National Automobile Chamber of Commerce to appoint a committee to promote automotive business in the U. S. and abroad. J. Walter Drake was made chairman, and, later that year, the Automotive Division of the Bureau of Foreign and Domestic Commerce in the Department of Commerce was organized, with Gordon Lee as the manager.

One of the innovations offered during the year was a

back-up lamp which was turned on automatically when the car was reversed. This was combined with the tail-lamp on the Wills-St. Claire.

On Dec. 9, Dr. Thomas Midgley, Jr. and associates proved effectiveness of tetraethyl lead in gasoline.

*1922* A new body style at the 1922 National Automobile Show was the roadster-coupe, primarily a business car, which consisted of a roadster body with a permanent top.

Balloon tires and air cleaners were introduced on passenger cars.

1922—The Peerless, one of the heavy cars of the 'twenties.

Ford bought Lincoln Motor Company at a receiver's sale and began production of higher-priced cars.

Durant bought Locomobile and Mason.

The earliest known electrically interlocked traffic signal system was installed in Houston, Texas.

Charles M. Schwab gained control of Stutz.

Elwood Haynes received the John Scott medal for metallurgical achievement in stainless steel, stellite, and chrome iron.

Several cars introduced a gasoline gauge on the instrument panel.

An Oldsmobile set a record, traveling 1,000 miles in 15 hours.

Automobile insurance policies were revised to cover the actual value rather than the purchase price of a car. Declining automobile prices led many insurance firms to believe motorists were deliberately destroying their cars to collect claims covering their depreciation on their automobiles.

In October Ford Motor Company astonished the automotive industry with a $50 reduction on all models.

Motor-driven snow removal equipment opened 27,096 miles of snow-covered highways from the East Coast through the Mid-West. This was the first concerted effort by many newly established state highway departments to use the motor truck in snow removal.

*1923* Most popular body styles at the 23rd National Automobile Show were the five-passenger closed car and the permanent-top phaeton. The four-door phaetons featured windows that lowered or could be removed for storage within the car.

Optimistic predictions over a peak production year proved correct. It was an all-time high record that stood until 1925. A total of 4,034,012 motor vehicles was sold by the manufacturers.

1923—The Star, Durant's bid for the light-car field, offered the first production station wagon.

Dodge offered steel closed bodies, in which sheet steel replaced wood everywhere except on the roof, which was an insert constructed of wood bows and slats covered by waterproof fabric.

Packard introduced the first mass-produced straight-eight L-head engines.

Springfield Body Corporation offered a factory-installed radio as optional equipment.

Zeder, Skelton, Breer Engineering Company joined Walter Chrysler, then board chairman of Maxwell-Chalmers Corp., to develop a new car to carry the Chrysler name.

Four-wheel brakes, foot-controlled headlamp dimmer switches and power-operated windshield wipers were adopted by several manufacturers as standard equipment.

"Ethyl" gasoline was first put on the market Feb. 2, in Dayton, Ohio, by General Motors Research Corporation.

Ford Motor Company announced a weekly purchase plan under which a customer was issued a coupon book and made at least $5 weekly payments to the local dealer. When

1923—The Rickenbacker bore the "hat-in-the-ring" insigne of the famous ace.

the total price of the car had been paid, the dealer delivered the car. The lowest price Model T was the runabout, selling at $265. (At the end of two years, more than 300,000 Ford cars were sold under the plan.)

With transmission gears locked in high, E. G. "Cannon Ball" Baker drove an Oldsmobile from New York to Los Angeles in 12½ days. The car was equipped with large gasoline tanks, and refueling enroute was accomplished by raising the rear wheels off the ground in order to keep the engine running.

Ford production exceeded two million cars during the year.

Alfred P. Sloan, Jr., became president of General Motors.

*1924* Not one electric, not one steamer, as the 24th National Automobile Show made the four-acre display at the 258th Field Artillery Armory the first 100 per cent gasoline National Automobile Show. Top mechanical attractions at the show were the increased number of cars featuring four-wheel brakes and balloon tires as standard equipment.

Six-cylinder vehicles were the most prized, a sensation being the Essex Coach priced under $1,000. Also of interest was the baked-enamel finish on low-priced cars.

The Chrysler light six, introduced by Maxwell-Chalmers Corp., featured a high-compression engine (4.5-to-1), seven-

1924—Flint Six touring car sported disc wheels and front bumper.

1924—Cars let families combine city living with country pleasures.

bearing crankshaft, four-wheel hydraulic brakes and a replaceable cartridge oil filter.

In addition to Packard and Duesenberg, straight-eight engines were offered by Auburn, Hupmobile, Jordan, Rickenbacker and several engine manufacturers.

General Motors Proving Ground at Milford, Mich., was completed.

Ethyl Corporation was organized by General Motors and Standard Oil (New Jersey).

The Winton Company discontinued manufacture of automobiles. Later, the firm was reorganized to produce Diesel engines.

Major Award Trophy was presented to the White Motor Company by the U.S.S.R. for reliability and endurance.

The publication "MoToR," edited 21 years for car owners, became a trade magazine.

Ford Motor Company produced its ten-millionth car.

There was now one automobile for every seven persons in the U. S.

A Reo motor bus made a transcontinental trip.

Two-filament bulbs, permitting use of direct and diverted light, appeared in headlights of some cars.

Nash Motors bought LaFayette Motors Corp.

Hudson announced its price on a coach which was $5 more than an open car.

Ford began manufacturing accessories for Ford cars.

Adoption of S.A.E. standards saved automobile manufacturers an estimated $124 for each car produced.

*1925* The most discussed mechanical aspect of new cars at the 25th National Automobile Show was the continued trend toward straight-eight engines. Balloon tires created the need for easier steering systems which were offered in 1925 models.

Other car features widely discussed were rumble seats, one-piece windshields, mohair upholstery and crank-type window lifts. Synthetic quick-drying pyroxylin finishes that could be sprayed on and baked gave the industry a wide range of colors in high-gloss finishes.

Accessories available to the automotive consumer included: balloon tire jacks, stop signals, locking radiator caps, trunk racks, all-weather enclosures for touring cars, mirrors, ash-trays, cigar lighters and heat indicators.

For the first time, more closed than open models were sold.

General Motors acquired control of the Yellow Truck and Coach Manufacturing Company.

Oldsmobile introduced chromium plating.

A.C.F. acquired Fageol Motors Company of Ohio and moved operations to Detroit.

General Motors Truck Company introduced a one-ton truck with four-wheel brakes.

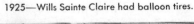

1925—Wills Sainte Claire had balloon tires.

Maxwell-Chalmers was reorganized as Chrysler Corporation.

Ford production exceeded 9,000 units a day.

Fisher Body acquired Fleetwood, a custom body-building company.

More than 150 electric railway systems were now operating motor buses.

Chrysler offered rubber engine mounts.

The 25-millionth U. S. motor vehicle was produced.

A national chain of drive-it-yourself stations was established.

Front and rear bumpers were now standard equipment.

Automobile Daily News began publication (later the name changed to Automotive News).

Uniform markings for Federal-aid highways were adopted. Even numbers were assigned to east-west roads, odd numbers to running north-south.

*1926* A feature of 1926 models at the 26th National Automobile Show was better vision, made possible by narrower pillars. Steel posts made this possible. Another windshield feature was the "shock-proof" glass offered by Stutz and Rickenbacker. The Stutz windshield had wire running horizontally through the glass at intervals of several inches, while the Rickenbacker windshield was a sandwich of transparent celluloid between two sheets of glass.

Other engineering features of the year included heavier crankshafts, shorter strokes and faster engines.

A novel car was the new Rickenbacker sport sedan, a low car with no running boards and a fender-mounted spare tire. The radiator, wire wheels, lamps and other exterior trim were brass finished, while the bumpers (shaped to resemble airplane propellers) were brass-bound mahogany. Gold plating was used on the interior hardware.

General Motors bought Fisher Body Corporation.
Ford inaugurated the five-day work week.
All outstanding Nash preferred stock was retired.
Dr. Graham Edgar devised the octane scale for gasoline.
Chandler offered a one-shot lubrication system.
Hot water car heaters were introduced in the U. S.

Edward "Ned" Jordan, president of the Jordan Motor Car Company, established a new trend in automobile advertising by shifting emphasis from technical details to the pleasures of driving. His ads, with eye-catching headlines such as "Somewhere West of Laramie," became famous.

Reo introduced the Flying Cloud models.

**1927** A definite trend toward the small car was apparent at the 27th National Automobile Show. In addition to the new Erskine, made by Studebaker, other

1927—Ford introduced the famous Model A.

## Somewhere West of Laramie

SOMEWHERE west of Laramie there's a broncho-busting,
steer-roping girl who knows what I'm talking about. She can
tell what a sassy pony, that's a cross between greased light-
ning and the place where it hits, can do with eleven hundred pounds
of steel and action when he's going high, wide and handsome.

The truth is—the Playboy was built for her.

Built for the lass whose face is brown with the sun when the day
is done of revel and romp and race.

She loves the cross of the wild and the tame.

There's a savor of links about that car—of laughter and lilt and
light—a hint of old loves— and saddle and quirt. It's a brawny
thing—yet a graceful thing for the sweep o' the Avenue.

Step into the Playboy when the hour grows dull with things gone
dead and stale.

Then start for the land of real living with the spirit of the lass who
rides, lean and rangy, into the red horizon of a Wyoming twilight.

# JORDAN

JORDAN MOTOR CAR COMPANY, Inc., Cleveland, Ohio

1926—A new style of auto-
mobile advertising was pioneered by the Jordan Motor
Car Company.

A few models had small glass "eyes" at the rear of the headlamps to enable the driver to see if his lights were on.

Three companion cars were introduced at the National Automobile Show. Ajax, a Nash-built six-cylinder car, and Moon's Diana had been on the road a few months earlier but the show was their first "public" appearance. Pontiac made by Oakland (General Motors) was first displayed at the industry-sponsored show.

E. G. "Cannon Ball" Baker drove a fully loaded two-ton GM truck from New York to San Francisco in record-breaking time of five days, 17 hours, 30 minutes.

Packard offered hypoid gears which permitted the propeller shaft to be lower, thus making it possible to lower the body line.

Ford announced plans to discontinue manufacturing the Model T.

small cars included the Little Marmon, in several models and styles; the Whippet and Whippet Six, made by Willys; and the Jordan Little Playboy. Four-wheel brakes were standard equipment on virtually all the cars at the show. Air cleaners, gasoline filters, crankcase ventilators, oil filters, automatic windshield wipers, balloon tires and rear-view mirrors were all becoming common.

The Packard and Little Marmon were equipped with hypoid rear axles, devised in response to demands for lower cars.

Cadillac introduced the LaSalle V-8.

The Fageol brothers organized the Twin Coach Company.

Mack adopted a vacuum brake booster and four-wheel brakes on trucks and fire engines.

Carl Breer began the study of aerodynamics in relation to automobile body design, which led to the "Airflow" design and monocoque type of body and chassis construction.

Graham-Paige Motors Corporation succeeded Paige-Detroit Motor Car Company.

Studebaker celebrated its Diamond Jubilee.

General Motors stockholders received $134,836,081 in dividends.

Nash announced that employees owned $20,000,000 worth of stock.

An electric drive with no gear shift was developed by E. M. Frazer.

Packard built a 500-acre proving ground with a two and one half-mile concrete oval test track at Utica, Michigan.

Ford produced the last (mass-produced) Model T on May 31. A total of 15,007,033 Model T's were assembled by the company since it was introduced in 1908. After a six-month changeover period, Ford introduced the Model A.

Chrysler shareholders received $10,000,000 in dividends.

Concrete mixers, mounted on White heavy-duty trucks, appeared on the Pacific Coast.

Lockheed (Malcolm Loughead) introduced an internal expanding hydraulic brake system.

*1928* Lower prices and an increase in the number of eight-cylinder cars were two predominant features of the new models in the 28th National Automobile Show. Higher compression ratios, combined with better fuel, brought about a higher horsepower average for the industry.

Cadillac introduced a synchromesh transmission, and safety plate glass in all windows.

Chandler offered Westinghouse vacuum brakes that reduced pedal pressure by two-thirds.

Most Graham-Paige models featured a four-speed transmission.

1928—Reo's Flying Cloud sport coupe with a rumble seat was typical of a popular body style of the later 1920's.

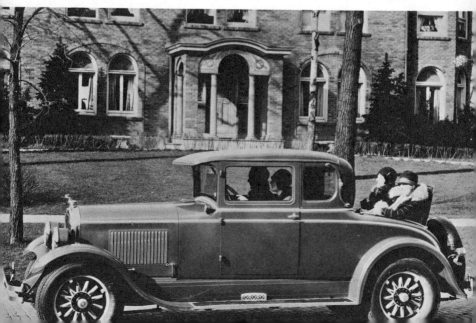

Chrysler purchased Dodge Brothers, Inc., July 30.

Studebaker acquired control of Pierce-Arrow.

Ford offered shatter-proof glass as standard equipment.

Coast-to-coast bus service began.

Brockway gained control of the Indiana Truck Corporation.

Buick celebrated its silver anniversary.

Chrysler entered the low-priced field with the Plymouth, and offered the De Soto as another new line of cars.

The publication "Fleet Owner" made its appearance.

Chevrolet reverted to six-cylinder engines instead of four's.

*1929* Public interest in new automobiles reached such heights that most Manhattan hotel lobbies were packed with displays of cars during the 1929 National Automobile Show. A number of redesigned models were first displayed at the show. Auburn had one streamlined

1929—The Marquette model 30 was introduced by Buick.

1929—The Viking with a V-8 engine was Oldsmobile's companion car.

aluminum model that resembled an airplane cabin; Franklin's *le Pirate* model concealed the running boards under the doors.

Hupmobile acquired two Chandler-Cleveland plants in Cleveland.

Kleiber Motor Company experimented with Diesel-powered trucks.

More than 80,000 De Sotos were sold during the first year of production.

Tail lamps on both sides of the car were introduced.

The Aerocar, a house trailer, provided a new form of transportation and mobile living.

Cord offered front-wheel drive.

Radios were offered as optional equipment on many automobiles.

Chrysler adopted a down-draft carburetor for better fuel distribution and increased efficiency.

Nash offered an eight-cylinder engine for the first time.

Ford raised its wage scale to $7-a-day minimum.

Companion cars were offered by two major manufacturers. Oldsmobile introduced the Viking, a V-8; Buick offered the Marquette.

Motor vehicle production broke all records in 1929. Output totaled 5,337,087 units (the greatest until 1949).

Almost 90 per cent of all American cars sold in 1929 were closed models (sedans, coaches, coupes, etc.), whereas almost 90 per cent sold in 1919 had been open models.


*1930* Confusion was apparent on prices of new models at the 30th National Automobile Show. Four makes had a higher price tag, while five other lines reduced prices.

Cadillac offered V-16 and V-12 engines. The new V-16 engine, rated at 185 horsepower, had a complete fuel system for each bank of cylinders, and a power brake operated by the manifold vacuum.

Studebaker introduced free-wheeling.

Graham-Paige offered rubber-cushioned chassis springs and aluminum pistons with Invar struts for reduced weight and added strength.

Chrysler offered an eight-cylinder engine for the first time.

The National Automobile Chamber of Commerce launched a plan which would withdraw 360,000 antiquated motor vehicles from use.

American Austin Car Company was organized to build the Austin Bantam.

Studebaker developed a carburetor intake silencer.

Cadillac, Chrysler, Dodge, LaSalle, Marmon and Roosevelt cars were wired for radio installation.

Pontiac developed tin plated pistons and pressed steel axle housing.

Plymouth franchises were given to all Chrysler, De Soto and Dodge dealers.

Police cars were being equipped with radios.

Cadillac offered automatic hydraulic tappet clearance adjusters.

1930—Cord featured a front-wheel-drive.

1930—Austin Bantam had a 75-inch wheelbase and was powered by a 14.8 horsepower four-cylinder engine.

1931—An unlimited number of custom-built body designs were available on standardized straight eight on Duesenberg chassis.

*1931* With all business still in decline, the 31st National Automobile Show reflected the automobile manufacturers' dilemma quite clearly: whether to risk vast sums on completely new models, or reduce drastically the prices of existing models. Most of the makers had the larger, more powerful, more luxurious cars that the public had signified it most wanted until the chill of the Great Depression had set in. They now offered these big cars at reduced prices.

During National Auto Show week, the National Automobile Chamber of Commerce passed a resolution favoring the grouping of new model announcements in November and December. This plan had a twofold aim: it was hoped that buying would be stimulated in the fall and winter, rather than have it create a rush every spring. By thus changing buying habits, it was hoped that the unhappy conditions of summertime rush and wintertime decline in factory work might be changed for the better.

The Oakland line of cars was discontinued in favor of its companion car, the Pontiac, which offered eight and six-cylinder models.

A GMC truck and refrigerated trailer delivered 21 tons of California fruit to New York in 117 hours running time—

1931—The double-cowl Packard phaeton was one of the luxury cars of the period. It has been considered by many as a "classic" car.

demonstrating the efficiency of the motor truck as practical for transporting perishable goods.

Plymouth offered "floating power" rubber engine mountings designed to give the engine an independent axis.

Buick adopted an eight-cylinder engine.

Free-wheeling was available on Auburn, Chrysler, De Soto, De Vaux, Dodge, Essex, Graham, Hudson, Hupmobile, Lincoln, Marmon, Peerless, Pierce-Arrow, Plymouth, Studebaker, Willys and Willys-Knight.

Oldsmobile adopted a synchromesh transmission.

Pontiac produced a radiator grille made of pressed steel.

The 50 millionth U. S. motor vehicle was produced during the year.

A retractable hardtop convertible was patented by B. B. Ellerbeck of Salt Lake City.

A standard warranty for passenger cars for 90 days or 4,000 miles, and 90 days and/or 5,000 miles for commercial vehicles was recommended by the National Automobile Chamber of Commerce directors.

*1932* The year opened in the gloomy economic climate of a deepening depression. It was destined to be the poorest auto production year since 1918. In general, the new models were heavier, but the power had not been increased correspondingly. Five makes displayed 12-cylinder models. Convertibles, both phaetons and coupes with disappearing tops, were popular at the exhibition.

Chrysler this year strove for silence with rubber-mounted engines and improvements to silence fans, air-intake and exhaust.

Ford offered a new model with a V-8 engine to replace the Model A.

Graham introduced full-skirted fenders.

Pierce-Arrow introduced hydraulic valve-lifters.

Buick, Cadillac, Chrysler, De Soto, Dodge and LaSalle offered vacuum-operated clutches. Nearly all other makes featured free wheeling, which could be engaged by a control on the dash of the car.

Inside visors began to replace outside shades in an effort to decrease wind-resistance.

Oldsmobile and Packard offered automatic chokes on their 1932 models.

Backed by Walter C. Marmon, Col. Arthur William Sydney Herrington, military transport engineer, began

1932—First year for the Ford V-8.

production of all-wheel-drive vehicles for lumber and petroleum industries.

White acquired Indiana Truck.

*1933* Aerodynamic streamlining was beginning to be noticed at the 33rd National Automobile Show. The skirted fender, V-front grille, sweeping tail lines, and slanted windshield were more prominent. Economy seemed to be important. Gasoline mileage was advertised by many manufacturers, and durability was stressed by nearly all companies.

Power brakes became available on a number of makes.

Fisher bodies offered "No-Draft Ventilation," with the front section of the side windows pivoted on the top and bottom to control the flow of air inside the car.

Use of the accelerator pedal for starting the engine was adopted on several makes to eliminate a separate starter pedal on the floor.

White developed a new type of bus, a coach with under-the-floor, horizontally-opposed 12-cylinder "pancake" engine.

Valve seat inserts, independent wheel suspension, and reflex glass tail- and stop-lights were introduced.

A drive-in theater was opened in Camden, N. J.

1933—Depression and the ravages of nature combined to drive thousands to pack their belongings on the car or in trailers and leave home for better opportunities.

1934—De Soto's Airflow model.

*1934* Two features that drew most attention at the 34th National Automobile Show were streamlining and the independent suspension of the front wheels. Streamlining was stressed in particularly by the new and quite revolutionary, De Soto and Chrysler "Airflow" models. Hupmobile and, to a degree, LaSalle also featured it. Nearly all cars had one of the three forms of independent front wheel suspension then shown.

Reo was the only car at the show with a completely automatic transmission, though several makers had automatic de-clutching devices. A low-priced Graham had a mechanical supercharger that forced air into the carburetor. Several makes had rear fender covers, then called "pants."

There was a noticeable trend to larger cars on the new models, even among those of lower price. Nearly all models were longer, wider and offered more room inside. Several were even wide enough to seat three persons comfortably in the front seat. Doors were made wider; on some models door openings were cut back over fenders to provide more room for entering and leaving the vehicle.

Chevrolet produced its 10-millionth car to celebrate its 23rd anniversary.

Chrysler and De Soto offered an automatic transmission overdrive on Airflow models.

The name of the National Automobile Chamber of Commerce was changed to the Automobile Manufacturers Association, Inc. (AMA).

Studebaker emerged from receivership.

Cadillac introduced a high output generator and voltage regulator to keep the battery fully charged for extra loads.

Reo offered a gear shift on the dash.

Radio controls, built into the instrument panel, appeared on several makes.

All General Motors cars—Cadillac, Buick, Oldsmobile, Pontiac and Chevrolet—offered the first production all-steel turret top in December for their line of 1935 models.

1935—The first Lincoln-Zephyr.

1935—Chevrolet pioneered the first all-steel station wagon body; it was on a panel delivery truck chassis.

*1935* The 35th National Automobile Show was sponsored by the Automobile Merchants Association of New York after the Automobile Manufacturers Association decided to wait until November for its show in an effort to stabilize employment.

Ford Motor Company, which had not participated in national shows since early in the century, took part in the 1935 show.

Hudson and Terraplane introduced a new "electric hand" fingertip control for gear shifting. The control was mounted on the steering column.

A trend toward lower-priced cars was noticed for the 1935 model year. New models, with fewer features or less power, were announced by Chrysler, De Soto, Graham, Hudson, Hupmobile, Packard, Pontiac and Reo—all with lower prices.

An AMA report disclosed that motorists paid one of every eight tax dollars.

A trend toward two-door and four-door sedans developed.

The Keeshin Transcontinental Run was conducted to give impetus to long-distance truck transportation.

Count Alexis de Sakhnoffsky designed streamlined trucks for White.

Ford introduced the Lincoln-Zephyr.

Nash offered a new type of "sealed-in" motor with the manifold cast inside the block.

Approximately 3 million automobiles now had radios.

Pontiac produced its one-millionth car.

Chevrolet adopted a new type of frame without the X-member.

The great break with tradition characterized the 36th National Automobile Show in November. Since it had been decided that a fall show would possibly help level the peaks and valleys in the industry's sales and employment, the manufacturers moved their new-model announcements ahead two months. The innovation won plaudits from the nation's leaders. President Roosevelt saluted the industry for its leadership in the "vanguard of recovery." Sales were encouragingly better than they had been at recent shows, some exhibitors jubilantly reported that they more than doubled.

The new 1936 model cars featured hand brakes on the left of the driver to give more room in the front seat. Nash exhibited a car with twin travel beds. A number of models provided more uncluttered room for front seat passengers by moving the hand brake to the driver's left.

*1936* Automobile manufacturers were optimistic that the buying spirit at the 1936 model introduction in the previous fall would carry through the year. It turned out to be the best year since 1929.

1936—House trailers, later to be known as mobile homes, brought nature as close as the highway from home.

The AMA reported that 95 per cent of all cars were sold under $750 wholesale.

The Department of Commerce announced that 54 per cent of all U. S. families owned cars.

Reo discontinued passenger car manufacturing to concentrate on a line of commercial vehicles.

The three-millionth Buick was built.

Hudson introduced a "radical safety control," a steel torque arm which resulted in easier steering and the elimination of "nosing down" when braking. Also offered on the Hudson was a double automatic emergency braking system with a separate reserve brake system that went into use in the event the primary brakes failed.

Sloping side windows and built-in defrosters appeared on many cars.

Nash Motors Company of Kenosha, Wis., merged with Kelvinator Corporation of Detroit to form Nash-Kelvinator

Corporation. Charles W. Nash became board chairman, and George W. Mason, president.

Exhibits at the 37th National Automobile Show in November were of a more popular nature with less technical and mechanical detail than in past years. Emphasis was on the comfort and beauty of new models. House trailers were also displayed at the show as an accessory for touring and camping.

## 1937

The Waterman Arrowbile was one of the earliest flying automobiles.

Buick made a new-model changeover in the record time of 10 days.

Chrysler spent $22 million in plant improvements, and built more than a million cars and trucks during the year.

Ford offered a choice of 60 h.p. and 85 h.p. engines.

Steering column gearshifts were offered by several manufacturers.

1937—Cord offered a supercharged front-wheel drive model.

Several of the cars on display at the 37th National Automobile Show, Oct. 27 through Nov. 3, featured the storage battery in a location under the hood, making it more accessible and near other regularly serviced items.

Oldsmobile and Buick introduced the Automatic Safety Transmission, an automatic gearshift.

Chrysler offered an adjustable seat that moved not only back and forth, but up and down as well. Chrysler cars also offered safety padding on the back of the front seat.

Windshield washers were offered by Studebaker.

*1938* The year saw one of the worst slumps in automotive history—production was down 40 per cent. New models for 1939 and the National Automobile Show in the fall were looked upon as the necessary stimulus to bring the automotive business out of its economic low.

Ford Motor Company introduced the Mercury line of cars. The new make was aimed for the medium price field, and equipped with a V-8 engine.

Studebaker spent $3.5 million in tooling for the new low-priced Champion model.

Nash introduced "conditioned air" heating and ventilation which heated and filtered fresh air from the outside, and then circulated it inside the car with a fan.

Packard offered "Econo-drive," an overdrive transmission.

Pontiac adopted "Duflex" rear springs that were used with a smaller auxiliary leaf spring for uniform riding quality under any load. A remote gearshift control on the steering column was also introduced.

Hudson introduced a 112-inch wheel-base model in the low-priced field.

Several manufacturers offered coil spring rear suspension in place of leaf springs.

1938—Plymouth offered a convertible top operated by vacuum power.

Chevrolet introduced a vacuum operated gearshift.

Chrysler developed "Superfinish," a method of finishing parts with no scratches more than one-millionth of an inch deep. The company also introduced a fluid coupling for the Chrysler transmission.

Ford spent $40 million for plant expansion.

New car models exhibited at the 39th National Automobile Show had several interesting features, including Buick's directional signals, and Plymouth's safety signal speedometer and vacuum operated convertible top.

Ford, Chevrolet and Dodge offered cab-over-engine trucks.

Dodge and International Harvester entered the Diesel-powered truck field.

*1939* Automotive production milestones were reached during the year. The 75 millionth motor vehicle was made in the U.S. Ford produced its 27 millionth vehicle, and the 15 millionth Chevrolet was produced.

Hudson introduced "Airfoam" cushions and a hood lock release under the dash.

White built 300 scout cars for the U.S. Army.

Packard designed and built a high-speed marine engine for the U. S. Navy's famous PT boats.

Powell Crosley, Jr. introduced the Crosley, a small car.

Nearly every manufacturer held its 1940 new car announcement until the 40th National Automobile Show in October, so the impact of the new models would be strong. The Show was held 27 days earlier than in past years to facilitate the group announcement.

There was a wide range of colors on the 1940 models exhibited at the National Automobile Show, and the colors were made more lustrous by the use of metallic pigments. Two-tones were displayed at many exhibits. The most popu-

1939—Powell Crosley, Jr. and the new Crosley car.

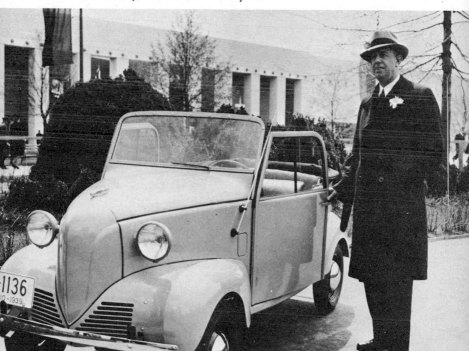

lar body style at the Show was the four-door six passenger sedan, followed by the two-door sedan. There was great spectator interest in the new station wagon models displayed.

Sealed Beam Headlamps were generally adopted for the first time by the automotive industry for the 1940 models.

Push-button radios appeared in cars.

Oldsmobile offered "Hydra-Matic Drive," an automatic transmission.

Automatic overdrive became available on several makes of cars. Lincoln-Zephyr and several models of other makes omitted running boards or enclosed them under the door.

Oldsmobile offered all-coil-spring suspension, four-way stabilization, and knee-action front-wheel suspension on all models.

Pontiac began production of taxi-cabs.

Several models featured an under-the-seat heater for better air circulation. Heaters and defrosters were standard equipment on many 1940 models.

An air condition unit was offered by Packard.

*1940* Col. Arthur W. S. Herrington invited a group of automotive engineers to Fort Benning, Ga., in March to witness demonstrations of a small armed vehicle designed and built by Capt. Robert G. Howie. This demonstration resulted in the development of the wartime one-quarter ton four-wheel-drive military vehicle, the forerunner of "Jeep" vehicles made by Willys Motors, Inc.

The war in Europe converted many U. S. automobile branch plants on the Continent to military production.

William S. Knudsen, president of General Motors, went to Washington at the invitation of President Roosevelt to direct production for national defense.

Nash introduced its "600" series, a pioneer of the mass produced unitized body.

1940—Oldsmobile offered Hydra-Matic automatic transmission as an accessory. Station wagons accounted for less than 1 per cent of total motor vehicles in the country.

Packard contracted to build Rolls-Royce aircraft engines.

Ford contracted to build Pratt & Whitney aircraft engines.

Dodge built 20,000 special trucks for the U. S. Army.

Chevrolet produced a million cars in less than ten working months.

Cadillac discontinued the LaSalle.

The 41st National Automobile Show in the Grand Central Palace Oct. 12–20, was the last of a series that had run without break from 1900. Before the event opened, AMA directors announced that all manufacturers had shelved plans for the 1941 show and new model introductions so that time and attention, as dictated by the emerging needs, could be devoted to production for national defense.

Ford Motor Company exhibited Ford, Lincoln and Mercury cars and Ford trucks for the first time in a National Auto Show sponsored by the AMA or its predecessors.

Hydra-Matic Drive was made available on all Cadillac models. Fluid Drive became available on Dodge, De Soto, and Chrysler cars.

Interchangeable six- or eight-cylinder engines on a basic frame were offered by Oldsmobile and Pontiac. A supporting radiator frame or longer fan shroud made up the difference in shorter engines.

Chrysler introduced a safety-rim wheel that kept the tire on the rim in the event of a blowout. Two-speed electric windshield wipers were also offered by Chrysler.

Buick offered a dual compound carburetor that cut in a second carburetor when the throttle was depressed to floor.

Enclosed running boards were generally adopted throughout the industry.

The Automotive Committee for Air Defense was established on Oct. 30 to facilitate aircraft production.

A nationwide plan for financing automotive repairs on an installment basis was announced.

*1941* Production records were made by at least three car makers. Plymouth made its 4 millionth unit, Dodge built its 5 millionth car and the 29 millionth Ford was produced.

The new 1942 models had a lower, longer, broader, and more massive look. Grilles were wider, bumpers heavier, and running boards were either absent or concealed.

Front fenders were extended to the middle of the front door on General Motors cars.

Hudson offered a combination automatic clutch with a

1941—The Nash Ambassador offered a folding seat which formed a bed.

semi-automatic transmission. The driver could select either the manual or semi-automatic shift with buttons on the dash.

Many makes substituted a lightweight iron alloy for pistons. Substitute materials were also used for trim and decoration.

De Soto's headlamps were concealed in the front fenders. The lamp doors disappeared upward when a knob under the instrument panel was pulled; this also turned on the lights.

*National Defense*

Buick built a new aviation engine plant.

Oldsmobile produced shells for the U. S. Army in a modern forge plant.

Chrysler achieved mass production of tanks, delivered its first anti-aircraft guns, and proceeded with scores of defense contracts.

Ford began production of combat cars.

Pontiac began work on Oerlikon anti-aircraft guns.

General Motors divisions began production of machine guns.

Studebaker took a contract to produce aircraft engines.

Willys started delivery of a reconnaissance car, soon to be popularly known as the "Jeep."

White produced half-tracks, tank destroyers, prime movers, and cargo trucks.

Naval forces from Japan struck Pearl Harbor Dec. 7—War against Japan was declared by the U. S. Congress on the following day.

The Automotive Council for War Production was organized on Dec. 31 to apply the full facilities of the automotive industry to the task of production for the armed forces.

1942—Military service and rationing put many automobiles into storage for the duration of World War II.

*1942* All automobile companies halted production of civilian passenger cars on Feb. 9.

Car rationing began March 2.

Production of civilian trucks halted March 3.

On May 3 the national speed limit was set at 40 m.p.h. to conserve fuel. It was later cut to 35 m.p.h.

Gasoline supplies were cut 50 per cent in 17 eastern states on May 15.

Also in May the Ford Willow Run Michigan Bomber Plant opened.

By July war output of automotive companies exceeded their peacetime production rate.

On Sept. 10 President Roosevelt ordered nation-wide gasoline rationing effective Dec. 1 to conserve fuel and rubber.

Graham-Paige began production of amphibian tanks.

Nash-Kelvinator produced Pratt & Whitney engines, Hamilton Standard propellers, Sikorsky helicopters.

Chrysler spent $40 million to increase tank production, and started a huge aircraft engine plant in Chicago.

Pontiac was the first automobile manufacturer to win the Navy "E" Award. When this award was superseded by Army-Navy "E," Chrysler Tank Arsenal was accorded the first such award in the U. S.

At the year's end the Automotive Council for War Production reported the industry's 1942 production of arms at $4,665,000,000.

*1943* The Office of Price Administration (O.P.A.) banned non-essential driving in 17 eastern states in January.

O.P.A. disclosed that 25 million gasoline ration books had been issued.

By June production for war in 1,000 automotive plants had doubled in 12 months; employment total: 1,250,000.

Henry Kaiser announced plans to manufacture automobiles after the war.

William B. Stout developed a "flying automobile" for postwar production.

By November employment in U. S. plants formerly manufacturing motor vehicles and bodies reached its wartime peak and began to taper off due to demands for manpower in armed services; output of such plants was now double the rate of best peacetime year.

The Automotive Council for War Production reported 1,038 automotive plants voluntarily cooperating in the industry-wide effort to maintain maximum production, and that value of products thus made had reached a total of $13 billion.

*1944* The War Production Board authorized production of 1,000,000 trucks for civilian and military use in 1944 in January.

Willys-Overland announced plans to produce a civilian version of the Jeep after the war.

The Detroit region was shown accountable for 13.6 per cent of the nation's war production.

The War Production Board announced formation of the Automobile Industry Advisory Committee to consider basic problems to be dealt with in eventual resumption of passenger car production.

Basic gasoline ration was reduced to two gallons a week.

Joseph W. Frazer, board chairman of Graham-Paige, announced plan to manufacture automobiles after the war.

In September the Office of War Information revaled that passenger cars were now being scrapped at the rate of 4,000 a day.

1943—Military vehicles rolled along assembly lines for the duration of the war.

1944—Automotive companies produced 57 per cent of the tanks delivered to U. S. and allied armed forces during World War II.

In November the War Production Board authorized manufacture of the first light civilian trucks since early in 1942.

It was revealed that the United States had supplied the U.S.S.R. with more than 345,000 motor vehicles.

The Automotive Council for War Production revealed that the automotive industry produced $9 billion worth of armament in 1944, and that costs to the Government had been reduced one-third since 1941.

## 1945

The Automobile Manufacturers Association statistics disclosed that 48 per cent of all passenger cars now in use were more than seven years old.

Crosley Corporation announced its intent to produce small cars powered with four-cylinder lightweight engines after the war.

1945—Henry Ford II drove the first civilian postwar automobile from the assembly line on July 3.

In April the War Production Board announced a program for transition to civilian motor vehicle production after V-E Day.

V-E Day became reality on May 8 when Germany surrendered to Allied Forces.

On May 11 the War Production Board announced that reconversion to motor vehicle production could begin July 1.

On May 22 all restrictions on manufacture of replacement parts were lifted.

Willow Run Plant closed on June 23 after delivering 8,685 bombers.

Ford began production of passenger cars on July 6.

Formation of Kaiser-Frazer Corporation was announced on July 26.

World War II ended with the surrender of Japan on Aug. 14.

Gasoline rationing ended the day following the Japanese surrender.

All restrictions on truck production were lifted on Aug. 20.

The Automotive Council for War Production was dissolved on Oct. 15.

Production of 1946 motor vehicles started. New models were announced by Chevrolet, Buick, Cadillac, Pontiac, Oldsmobile, Studebaker, Nash, Hudson and Packard.

A strike began in General Motors plant on Nov. 21.

## SUMMARY OF AUTOMOTIVE INDUSTRY'S WAR PRODUCTION

The automotive industry contributed more material to the armed services of the United States and Allies than any other single industry. In addition to all the armored cars used, it supplied 92 per cent of the scout cars and carriers, 87 per cent of the aircraft bombs, 85 per cent of the steel

113

helmets, 75 per cent of the aircraft engines, 57 per cent of the tanks, 56 per cent of the carbines, 50 per cent of the Diesel engines, 47 per cent of the machine guns, 10 per cent of the completed aircraft, 10 per cent of the torpedoes, 10 per cent of the land mines, and 3 per cent of the marine mines.

By the end of the war, almost $29 billion worth of products for war had been delivered. This total was approximately 20 per cent of the national output of such products.

*1946* Kaiser and Frazer joined the ranks of U. S. passenger car manufacturers in offering new models bearing their names.

A corporation to build Preston Tucker's rear-engine car was organized with $40 million capitalization. The firm leased the Chicago-Dodge plant during the latter part of the year.

Despite a coal strike that impeded automotive produc-

1946—Studebaker pioneered a trend in post-war styling.

1946—The Crosley entered the small car field after World War II.

tion, the one-millionth passenger car assembled since the end of World War II was built in August.

A 12-day celebration in Detroit from May 29 through June 9 marked the Automotive Golden Jubilee.

Radio telephones were used in motor vehicles.

Disabled veterans could obtain cars equipped with special mechanical aids developed by the Society of Automotive Engineers.

Power operated windows were introduced.

Chevrolet Division was one of the first automotive firms to advertise on network television.

The Public Roads Administration removed all restrictions on Federal Aid highway construction not requiring structural steel.

Price and wage controls were lifted by the Federal Government on the automotive industry on Nov. 9.

Studebaker offered self-adjusting brakes.

Willys-Overland Motors, Inc., introduced a seven-passenger Jeep all-steel station wagon.

*1947* Motor vehicle manufacturers built and purchased a number of new plants. General Motors opened a new assembly plant in Wilmington, Delaware; Studebaker bought a wartime aircraft engine plant at South Bend; and Chevrolet opened new passenger car and truck assembly plants in Flint, Michigan and Van Nuys, California.

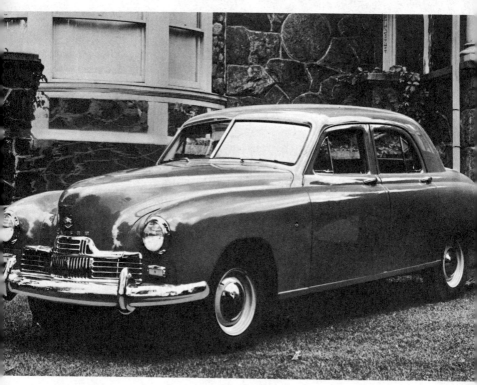

1947—The Kaiser was the low-priced car made by Kaiser-Frazer Corp.

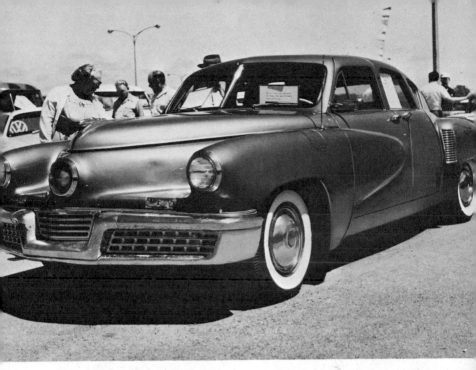

1947—A few Tucker "48" pilot models were produced for public displays around the country. The Tucker had a rear engine and a third headlamp which turned with the front wheels.

Kaiser-Frazer Corporation purchased the automotive assets of the Graham-Paige Motor Corporation.

Sun visors outside the windshield appeared again as accessories. The trend for such visors had declined during the early thirties.

Packard produced its one millionth car and offered power-operated windows and seat adjustment.

Driver education courses were offered in many high schools.

Tucker Corporations' Torpedo (later called the "48") was unveiled in Chicago.

*1948* Because there had not been a National Show since 1940, each automotive firm offered its new models when they were ready.

Willys-Overland introduced a six-cylinder Jeep station wagon and a convertible called the Jeepster.

Goodrich introduced tubeless tires.

Under the direction of Charles F. Kettering, General Motors revealed development of a new type of high-compression engine that was designed to use high-octane fuel.

The 100-millionth motor vehicle was produced in the U. S. during August.

Oldsmobile opened a new plant especially tooled to manufacture its new high compression V-8 engines.

Buick introduced Dynaflow transmission, a hydraulic torque converter.

Kaiser-Frazer bought the Willow Run plant near Ypsilanti, Michigan.

Cadillac, Buick and Oldsmobile offered double curved windshields.

The American trucking industry celebrated its 50th anniversary.

Pontiac offered Hydra-Matic drive as optional equipment.

New motor vehicle assembly plants were opened on the East and West Coasts: General Motors at Wilmington, Delaware and Framingham, Massachusetts, Lincoln-Mercury at Los Angeles, and Dodge Division at San Leandro, California.

Great Britain, Canada and the United States signed an agreement for standardization of threads on screws, nuts and bolts. This became known as the A.B.C. thread standard.

Tucker Corporation reported completion of its first assembly line model.

More than 1,000 dual-control cars were loaned by automotive companies to high schools in the U. S. for training student drivers.

1947—Chrysler offered a Town and Country series that combined features of a station wagon and convertible.

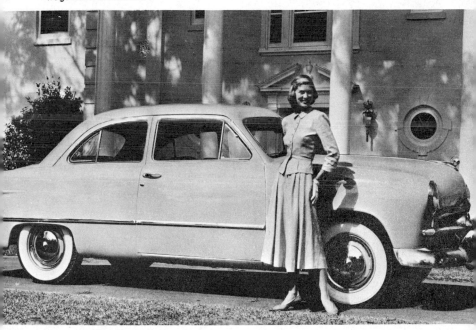

1948—Styling and engineering changes in the 1949 model Ford were extensive. It was the first completely new design for Ford since the end of World War II.

Most 1949 model American-made cars were introduced to the public in the fall.

Three new cars were offered—Playboy, Keller and Davis.

1949—Buick introduced a hardtop convertible which became a popular body style.

## 1949

General Motors' first show since 1940, "Transportation Unlimited," opened in New York.

Kaiser-Frazer introduced three new body styles—a utility car, a taxicab and a cloth-covered hardtop sports sedan.

Cadillac offered a high compression V-8 engine with hydraulic valve lifters.

Bonded brakes were adopted by Dodge (light trucks), Chevrolet, Chrysler and Crosley.

Oldsmobile introduced its new "88" series with a high compression V-8 engine.

Ford Division was organized to assemble and market Ford cars and trucks.

Dodge introduced an inexpensive three-passenger roadster, the Wayfarer—the first car of this body style since before World War II.

Buick, Oldsmobile and Cadillac started production of their hardtop (a sedan without center pillars) models, the Riviera, Holiday and Coupe de Ville respectively.

Hupp Corporation announced plans to sell its Detroit plant and apply funds to expansion elsewhere.

Government controls on automobile installment credit (Regulation W) limiting financing to 24 months ended June 30.

De Soto introduced a nine-passenger station wagon.

Willys-Overland introduced a new four-wheel drive all-steel station wagon as part of the Jeep series.

Plymouth introduced the Suburban, a steel station wagon.

Chrysler adopted a new method of starting the engine by using only the ignition key.

1949—Cadillac introduced a high compression V-8 engine with hydraulic valve lifters. The engine was one of the first postwar designs offered to the motoring public.

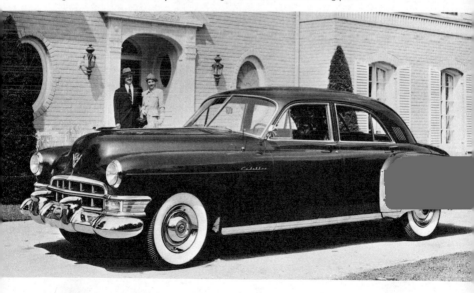

Kurtis-Kraft, Inc., racing car manufacturer, entered the passenger car field with the announcement of a low-slung convertible sports car.

Steel and coal strikes forced production curtailment at auto plants in the fall.

Crosley introduced a new sports car, the Hotshot.

Ford and Studebaker contracted with Borg-Warner for a new automatic transmission.

Tucker Corporation was ordered by the Federal Court to return its leased Chicago plant to the War Assets Administration.

Nearly all U. S. passenger car manufacturers offered their 1950 models in the fall. Some of the new features included Powerglide automatic transmission on the Chevrolet, Hydra-Matic on some Nash models, and hydraulically-operated valves on the Cadillac, Oldsmobile and Buick.

White Motor Co. introduced several new features for its line of trucks, including a hydraulically-operated tilting cab and Hydro-Torque Drive transmission.

The American Trucking Associations reported that trucks carried about 60 per cent of the total freight tonnage moved in the nation's commerce.

As the year ended, the automotive industry broke its own 20-year-old annual record to hit an all-time high of 6,253,651 units.

*1950* Nash-Kelvinator displayed the NXI, a two-passenger experimental car, as part of a survey of public reaction to a new light car. As a result of the findings, the firm introduced the Metropolitan in 1954.

Many of the 1950 cars had reduced prices.

Hardtop models were offered by Chevrolet, Chrysler, Dodge and De Soto.

1950—Nash Rambler with 100-inch wheel-base.

Crosley introduced the Super Sports model, priced to sell for less than $1,000.

At least two new lines of trucks were offered during the year. Dodge introduced a four-ton model, and White offered two new "Super Power" trucks.

Reo started production of the Eager Beaver, a 2½-ton truck, for the U. S. Army.

The three-millionth Oldsmobile was produced in February. In October Oldsmobile discontinued its six-cylinder engine to concentrate output on the Rocket V-8 engine.

Goodrich offered puncture-sealing tubeless tires.

Marmon-Herrington Co., Inc., bought the manufacturing rights to Ford motor coaches.

Nash-Kelvinator introduced the Rambler series, and offered seat belts.

Chrysler celebrated its 25th anniversary, and Mack held its golden anniversary in June.

Hostilities in Korea started June 25.

Nearly all automotive companies were awarded military contracts for defense products.

U. S. Department of Defense revealed plans for the reactivation of an Ordnance Tank-Automotive Center in Detroit to expedite mobilization of the automotive and allied industries.

Installment credit was tightened for new and used cars to 15 months with one-third down.

Crosley introduced a farm and road vehicle, the Farm-O-Road, with a 10-to-1 compression ratio engine.

Willys built a small engine for Kaiser-Frazer's Henry J car, which was displayed in September.

Several 1951 models were introduced in the fall. Some of the new features included: V-8 engines and automatic transmissions on Studebaker models; one-piece curved windshields; plastic-insulated ignition system to guard against moisture on the Nash; tinted non-glare glass on the Buick; automatic transmission on Ford (Fordomatic) and Mercury (Merc-O-Matic); crash pads on the Kaiser; and an all-steel station wagon for Chrysler (Town and Country).

Chevrolet produced its 25-millionth vehicle in December.

As the year ended, material shortages resulting from the military build-up caused temporary shutdowns in automotive assembly plants.

*1951* Civilian use of nickel, zinc and tin was ordered cut by the Federal government. Automotive companies used new methods and materials in producing car components as a result of the government cutback.

By the first part of the year most automotive companies had already received, or were in the process of negotiating, military contracts for the Korean conflict.

The National Production Authority halted the shipment of spare tires in new automobiles. Later in the year this ban was lifted.

Several new models were added this year. Ford offered a hardtop model—the Victoria, Lincoln introduced the customized Capri, Plymouth offered the Belvedere hardtop, Kaiser offered four new utility models, Nash added the two-passenger Nash Healey sports car (built by the Donald Healey Co. of England), a hardtop model was added to the Nash Rambler series, Packard added the Mayfair hardtop model to its line of cars, and Oldsmobile introduced the Super 88.

Buick displayed its XP 300 experimental car with a 300 horsepower V-8 supercharged engine. General Motors exhibited the Le Sabre experimental convertible, and Chrysler displayed its K-310 experimental car.

General Motors added 1,000 acres to its Milford Proving Ground to facilitate testing military vehicles.

1951—Increased emphasis was placed on all-steel station wagons by nearly all manufacturers, including Willys.

1951—Oldsmobile introduced the "Super 88" series which featured a new body design combined with a high compression V-8 engine.

Cadillac produced its first T41 Walker Bulldog light tank and Chrysler completed a pilot model of the T43 heavy tank.

Ford offered a six-cylinder engine with overhead valves.

Continental Motors acquired rights to nine gas turbine engines developed by Societé Turbomeca in France.

Buick offered a V-8 engine on some models.

Power steering was offered by Chrysler and Buick.

Oldsmobile offered a watch mounted in the steering wheel.

Sterling Motor Truck Company stockholders approved the sale of its business to the White Motor Company.

Automobile installment credit was extended to 18 months with one-third down payment.

General Motors Truck and Coach Division displayed its new Army 6 × 6 truck, the M135.

The Internal Revenue Act of 1951 increased automotive excise taxes from 5 to 8 per cent on trucks, 7 to 10 per cent on passenger cars, and 5 to 8 per cent on automotive parts and accessories.

Willys-Overland Motors, Inc., introduced its first postwar six-cylinder passenger car, the Aero Willys.

Kaiser-Frazer suspended production of the Frazer car.

Sears, Roebuck and Company introduced the new Kaiser-Frazer made Allstate passenger car. The car was displayed in 19 cities in the South and Southwest a week before Christmas.

Michigan State College (later, University) established a driver-training professorship.

The 100,000,000th passenger car built in the U. S. was assembled in December.

*1952* The year marked important milestones for two automotive companies. Studebaker celebrated its 100th anniversary and Cadillac marked its golden anniver-

1952—Sears, Roebuck and Co., offered the Allstate. The car, a version of the Henry J made by Kaiser-Frazer, was available with four or six-cylinder engine.

sary. The American Automobile Association (AAA) celebrated its 50th anniversary, and the U. S. Post Office issued a commemorative stamp honoring the 50th anniversary of the trucking industry in the U. S.

Some innovations offered on 1952 models included: Oldsmobile's automatic headlamp dimmer; a suspended brake pedal under the dashboard and ball joint front wheel suspension on the Lincoln; suspended clutch and brake pedals on the Ford; dual range Hydra-Matic on the Pontiac; 12-volt electrical system on the Chrysler Crown Imperial; four way seat adjustment on the Packard; automatic overdrive on the Plymouth; and De Soto offered a V-8 engine.

International Harvester and Reo introduced a liquefied-petroleum gas (LPG) powered line of motor trucks.

GMC offered a 2.5-ton, three-cylinder, diesel truck.

The last nine miles were opened on New Jersey's 118-mile turnpike in January.

Operation of the Detroit Tank Aresenal was transferred to Chrysler Corporation.

General Tire and Rubber bought Crosley Motors in July; production of the Crosley car stopped during the same month.

Dodge and Fisher Body used plastic dies to produce steel stampings for automotive components.

Automotive companies continued to produce military goods for the Korean conflict. In addition to military motor vehicles and tanks, they built aircraft engines, jet and piston type; electronic aircraft gun sights; diesel marine engines; aircraft; and a number of miscellaneous components for weapons.

Hudson introduced a new low-priced car in September, the Jet.

University of Michigan formed a Transportation Institute within the College of Engineering to encourage better understanding of the need for more efficient transportation.

Willys-Overland Motors added the Aero Ace and Aero Lark to its Aero series of passenger cars.

Dearborn Motors Corporation paid $9,250,000 to Harry Ferguson, Inc. in settlement of a judgment which ended the Ford-Ferguson tractor patents litigation.

Buick offered the Skylark deluxe convertible in the $5,000 price bracket.

Lincoln-Mercury Division of Ford Motor Company moved into its new assembly plant at Wayne, Michigan, a Detroit suburb, for production of the division's two cars.

The U. S. Chamber of Commerce estimated that private automobiles carried about 85 per cent of the nation's combined local and long distance traffic.

Chrysler Corp. started construction on its 3,800-acre proving ground at Chelsea, Michigan.

*1953* Four significant milestones in the automotive industry were passed during the year. Buick and Ford Motor Company celebrated their golden anniversaries; the Automobile Manufacturers Association, Inc., noted its 40th anniversary; and Plymouth celebrated its 25th year.

Kaiser-Frazer changed its name to Kaiser Motors Corporation. In April, Kaiser purchased Willys-Overland Motors, Inc.

White Motor Company purchased Autocar Company and announced plans for a $2 million Autocar plant at Exton, Pennsylvania.

General Motors dedicated its new 2,280-acre Desert Proving Ground near Phoenix, Arizona.

Six experimental cars were displayed by U. S. auto makers during 1953. Buick had the Wildcat; Lincoln-Mercury displayed its fiberglas body XL-500; Packard unveiled the Balboa; Hudson introduced the Italia; Dodge exhibited the handbuilt Firearrow; and De Soto showed a four-passenger sports car, the Adventurer.

Motor vehicles were used in an atomic bomb test in Nevada during March to determine the effects for civilian defense data.

General Motors purchased the outstanding stock in the Euclid Road Machinery Company.

Ford Motor Company purchased a 177-acre site at Mahwah, New Jersey for a Ford Division assembly plant.

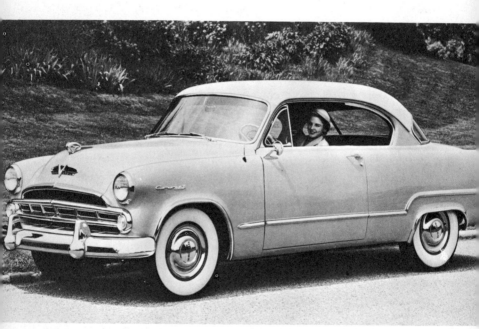

1953—Dodge offered a V-8 engine. It was the first year in U. S. automotive history that more eight than six-cylinder engines were produced.

Chevrolet announced plans to add 160,000 square feet to its Cleveland plant.

White sold its Milwaukee plant, formerly owned by the Sterling Motor Truck Company.

1953—Air suspension was offered in GMC transit coaches to give a more comfortable ride and reduce maintenance time.

Chrysler Corporation purchased the automotive plants and machinery of the Briggs Manufacturing Company.

The Korean truce agreement was signed at Panmunjom, July 26.

A multi-million-dollar fire destroyed the General Motors Transmission plant in Livonia, Michigan on August 12, cutting off production of Hydra-Matic transmissions. Until other facilities could be arranged, Cadillac and Oldsmobile used Dynaflow transmissions and Pontiac adapted Powerglide units as optional equipment. Hydra-Matic production operations were shifted to another plant until General Motors purchased the Willow Run assembly plant from Kaiser Motors for automatic transmission output.

Radio Corporation of America (RCA) announced the development of safety electronic steering and braking controls which would stop or change the course of a car when an obstacle was in the path of the vehicle.

Production started on Chevrolet's plastic laminated fiberglas body sports car, the Corvette.

An American Automobile Association study showed that the average motorist drove 10,000 miles a year and paid about $908 for car maintenance and operation.

Features offered in 1953 included: Air conditioning on a number of makes; automatic transmissions on nearly all cars as optional equipment, and standard equipment in more expensive models; 12-volt electrical system, to replace 6-volt systems; lamps to replace oil pressure and generator gauges in several makes; and tinted, plexiglass roofs on some hardtop models.

Hydra-Matic transmissions became available on GMC trucks.

With the popularity of V-8 engines, the number of eight-cylinder engines exceeded the six-cylinder power plants in new passenger cars for the first time.

## 1954

Several long-established automotive companies merged. Nash-Kelvinator Corporation and Hudson Motor Car Company combined into American Motors Corporation; Studebaker Corporation and Packard Motor Car Company formed Studebaker-Packard Corporation.

Nearly all automotive companies announced major expansion programs. Research facilities and assembly plants received the largest share of capital expenditures. General Motors announced it would spend over $1 billion in two years; Chrysler worked out a 100-year loan of $250 million with Prudential Insurance Company of America for expansion and modernizations; and Ford invested millions in property and construction for future needs.

The Automotive History Collection of the Detroit Public Library was opened to the public in February. Some of the acquisitions of automobiliana in the Collection included: Charles B. King Collection, Andrew Lee Dyke Collection, and the Nicholas Lazarnick Picture Collection. The Automobile Manufacturers Association, and others, donated funds for the purchase of many important acquisitions in the Automotive History Collection.

Eight experimental cars were introduced during the year—Dodge's Granada; Packard's fiberglas sports model, the Panther; a gas turbine-powered XP-21 Firebird by General Motors; the Belmont and Explorer by Plymouth; Lincoln-Mercury's Monterey XM-800; the FX-Atmos dream car by Ford; and De Soto's Adventurer II.

Packard adopted tubeless tires as standard equipment in June. By the end of the year, all other U. S. manufacturers offered tubeless tires as original equipment.

The first section of New York State's $962 million Thruway system opened June 24.

A gas turbine engine developed by Chrysler Corporation was installed in a regular production Plymouth passenger car and successfully road tested. The test demonstrated the solution to two major problems in gas turbine engineering—high fuel consumption and exhaust heat—which had previously blocked passenger car application of gas turbine power.

1954—Buick offered the Century series. Power windows and power front seat were standard equipment on the convertible.

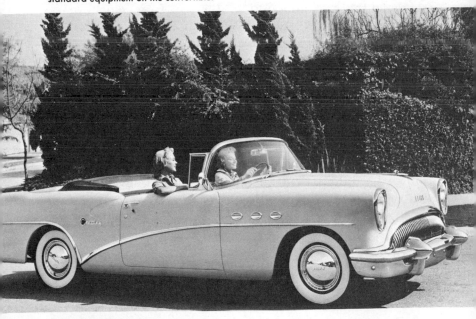

Ford introduced the two-passenger Thunderbird in October.

All automotive manufacturing in American Motors was moved to Kenosha, Wisconsin.

Ford Motor Company purchased 4,000 acres of land near Romeo, Michigan for development of a multi-million-dollar proving ground. Chrysler dedicated its new Engineering Proving Ground near Chelsea, Michigan.

Kaiser Motors Corporation transferred Willys body operations from Detroit to Toledo, Ohio.

Improved Sealed Beam headlamps, developed cooperatively through engineering committees of the Automobile Manufacturers Association and lamp manufacturers, were demonstrated. The new headlamps were on all new U. S. passenger cars by the middle of 1955.

West Virginia's new 88-mile turnpike was opened on Nov. 8.

A 22-mile section of the Northern Ohio Turnpike opened to the public on Dec. 1, linking Youngstown, Ohio with the Pennsylvania Turnpike.

Louis Matter of San Diego, California and two friends completed the first non-stop motor trip from Anchorage, Alaska to Mexico City, Mexico a distance of 6,391 miles.

General Motors Corporation produced its 50 millionth car.

President Dwight D. Eisenhower authorized the creation of a permanent President's Action Committee for Highway Safety.

New features offered by car makers during 1954 included panoramic wrap-around windshields; safety padding on dash boards; cowl ventilator air intakes at the bottom of the windshield; automatic transmission selector lever on the dash of Chrysler Corporation cars; dual headlamps and curved glass side windows on the Cadillac-El Camino; V-8 engines for Plymouth and Chevrolet; overhead valves for all

Ford car and truck engines; and push button control for lubrication of chassis and suspension on the Mercury and the Lincoln.

*1955* The automotive industry broke all records in motor vehicle production during 1955. Output totaled 9,204,049 units, including 7,950,377 passenger cars, 1,249,576 trucks and 4,096 motor coaches.

Ford Motor Company announced plans to build a glass manufacturing plant at Nashville, Tennessee and moved assembly operations from Edgewater to Mahwah, New Jersey; Chrysler Corporation bought Universal Products Company, makers of automotive drive shafts and their components; Plymouth opened its new V-8 engine plant in

1955—Continental Mark II.

1955—Packard 400 hardtop featured a "Torsion-Level" ride which dispensed with coil or leaf springs.

Detroit; Chrysler announced plans to construct a large stamping plant at Twinsburg, Ohio; and General Motors automotive divisions added to their plant facilities.

Newcomers to the automotive field were Tri-Car, Inc., with a three-wheeled plastic body model selling for about $1,000, and Dual Motors Corporation of Detroit with a limited production sports car, the Firebomb, with a Ghia-built body from Italy on a U. S. produced chassis.

Kaiser and Willys announced plans to drop passenger car production to concentrate on Jeep vehicles.

Kaiser Motors Corporation was reorganized as Kaiser Industries Corporation, with Willys Motors, Inc., a wholly owned subsidiary.

Slick Airways, Inc., pioneered truck-air-truck shipments with door-to-door freight service with overnight deliveries from coast to coast.

The U. S. Department of Commerce announced plans to conduct a road test near Ottawa, Illinois to determine the durability of several methods of highway construction. Cooperating with funds, personnel, and equipment were: Bureau of Public Roads, American Association of State Highway Officials, Department of Defense, Automobile Manufacturers Association, petroleum industry and other allied fields.

Improved Sealed Beam headlamps were installed in all new passenger cars by July.

Ohio's 241-mile turnpike was opened from the Pennsylvania Turnpike to west of Montpelier, Ohio on Oct. 1.

Safety door latches to help prevent doors from being forced open in collisions were made standard equipment on nearly all makes. Vehicle manufacturers also increased emphasis on seat belts.

Michigan was the first state to require a course in driver education before licenses could be issued to youths under 18.

Four-door hardtop models, offered by several manufacturers, became the vogue in body style.

Experimental vehicles displayed during the year were: Chevrolet's Biscayne, the Strato-Star by Pontiac, Oldsmobile's Delta, the Wildcat III from Buick, Cadillac's Eldorado Brougham, the V-6 powered LaSalle II by General Motors, Chrysler Corporation's Flight Sweep I and II along with the Falcon, Ford's plastic Mystere, General Motors' Firebird II gas turbine car, Ford's Futura—a $250,000 laboratory on wheels, and the Universelle truck by General Motors Coach and Truck.

Ford Motor Company's Continental Mark II was introduced at most Lincoln dealerships in October.

Studebaker entered the sports car field with the Hawk in November.

American Motors offered a V-8 engine in the Ambassador line; Packard introduced a V-8 along with torsion bar suspension controlled by a motor; and Chevrolet added the Nomad model at the top of its station wagon line.

137

The American Automobile Association stopped sanction of automobile races.

Cadillac offered a trunk lid lock control operated from the driver's seat.

A push-button, automatic-transmission selector replaced lever controls on the steering columns of 1956 model Chrysler, Imperial, De Soto, Dodge, Plymouth and Packard cars. A record player was also optional on Chrysler Corporation cars. Packard offered electrically-controlled door-latches and a non-slip differential.

The Motor Truck Committee of the Automobile Manufacturers Association reported completion of an auxiliary braking system designed to provide positive emergency stopping for truck-trailer combinations.

*1956* Ford Motor Company stock was offered to the public for the first time; more than 10 million shares owned by the Ford Foundation were offered at $64.50 per share. At the first public stockholders' meeting in May, Ford officials announced a $592 million expansion program for 1956.

A new Dual Headlighting System for motor vehicles was announced by the Automobile Manufacturers Association. Scheduled for introduction by the automotive industry for the 1958 models, the system comprised four 5¾-inch Sealed Beam headlamps instead of two 7-inch units. This enabled the headlamps to be aimed for the best individual performance.

Armco Steel Company purchased the grounds and buildings of the American Bantam Company; the remaining assets were bought by Pressed Metals of America, Inc.

Chevrolet entered the heavy duty truck field with a new line of 2½-ton models.

Dual Motors Corp. changed the name of its car from Firebomb to Dual-Ghia.

General Motors displayed a free-piston engine which burned any type of fuel—from high octane gasoline to whale oil, peanut oil and other vegetable fats.

A 41,000 mile interstate highway system was approved as a result of the Highway Act of 1956. The law committed the federal government to meet 90 per cent of the cost with states and localities supplying the remainder. The highway program was set up on a "pay-as-you-go" basis with the establishment of a Highway Trust Fund supported by highway use taxes to finance the federal share. Federal gasoline and diesel oil taxes were increased one cent on July 1 when the Highway Act became effective.

Mack Truck, Inc., acquired C. D. Beck and Company, Inc., an intercity bus manufacturer in Sidney, Ohio, and the sales, service and manufacturing facilities of Brockway Motor Company, Inc., an early truck manufacturer.

Divco Corporation changed its name to Divco Truck Division of Divco-Wayne Corporation.

1956—A 41,000-mile national network of super highways was started under a $32.4 billion interestate highway program.

Ford Motor Company joined the Automobile Manufacturers Association, Inc.

Production of the Packard car in Detroit stopped at the end of the 1956 model year; all operations were transferred to Studebaker-Packard Corporation's plants in South Bend, Indiana.

The 156-mile Northern Indiana Toll Road was opened Sept. 18. It crossed the state from Gary, at the west edge of Indiana, to the western terminal of the Ohio Turnpike, completing a toll system and enabling motorists to drive from the Chicago area to New York City on super-highways.

Chrysler Corporation's gas turbine powered experimental Plymouth was driven from New York to Los Angeles.

American Motors Corporation developed a 62-horsepower V-4 air-cooled engine that weighed 200 pounds.

The 42nd National Automobile Show, first since 1940, was held in New York's new Coliseum. More than 300,000 square feet of exhibition space on three floors were filled with 1957 car and truck models, and a musical revue was presented on a huge stage. All American passenger cars were displayed along with 11 truck and bus exhibits. It was the first time a National Automobile Show was televised—an estimated 21,600,600 people, in 115 communities across the nation, saw the hour-long network show. The speaker at the industry's traditional banquet was Vice President Richard M. Nixon, who delivered the first major foreign policy address ever made by a vice president of the United States.

New features on the 1957 models displayed at the National Auto Show included: torsion bar suspension on Chrysler Corporation cars; fuel injection was optional on the Rambler, Pontiac and Chevrolet; dual headlamps on some makes; rear facing seats in nine-passenger Plymouth station wagons; 14-inch wheels on three-quarters of the 1957 makes; curved side window glass on the Imperial; retractable rear window controlled from the dash on the Mercury; the Turbo-glide automatic transmission (three turbines and planetary gears with a hill retarder) on the Chevrolet; a metal top retractable convertible was introduced by Ford; six-way power seats were offered by several manufacturers; electric door locks were offered by several luxury lines; a speedometer buzzer which sounded when a pre-set speed was reached; and a non-slip differential was offered by several manufacturers.

## 1957

Historic and production milestones for the year included Oldsmobile's 60th anniversary, Pontiac's golden anniversary (founded as the Oakland Motor Car Company), International Harvester's 50th anniversary as a truck producer, the Automotive Safety Foundation's 20th anniversary, Plymouth's 10-millionth car, and the three-millionth Mercury.

The Bureau of Public Roads approved 85 miles of the Kansas State Turnpike for inclusion in the Interstate Highway System.

1957—Rambler station wagons featured a roof travel rack.

1957—Ford introduced a retractable hardtop convertible.

1957—Plymouth had a low silhouette, and featured a torsion bar front suspension system.

142

White Motor Company purchased the assets of Reo Motors, Inc., of Lansing, Michigan, a pioneer automotive firm.

A station wagon body was offered on the Packard Clipper —the first of this style for Packard since 1950.

Studebaker offered a low-priced economy model with minimum trim details, the Scotsman.

Mack Trucks, Inc., introduced a 41-passenger cross-country luxury bus.

The board of directors of the Automobile Manufacturers Association, Inc., at its annual June meeting adopted a resolution to exclude speed and racing from automotive advertising and publicity.

Ford production of its two-passenger Thunderbird stopped to prepare for a four-passenger model.

Nash and Hudson names were dropped by American Motors Corporation with the end of the 1957 model. The firm announced its 1958 cars would be part of the Rambler line.

The five-mile Mackinac Bridge, linking the two Michigan peninsulas, opened in November. Before the bridge was built motorists used state-operated ferry boats to cross the Straits of Mackinac.

Chevrolet and General Motors Truck and Coach Division displayed an experimental turbine-powered truck, the Turbo-Titan.

Ford Motor Company developed an aluminum experimental military vehicle with unitized construction. The company also displayed an experimental truck powered by a gas turbine engine.

One new car make and a number of features were offered for the 1958 model year. The Dual Headlamp System (four lamps) was adopted by nearly all makes. Ford Motor Company introduced the Edsel, which had self-adjusting brakes, push button automatic transmission in the center of the steering wheel, a floating drum-type speedometer, and a single air conditioner and heater control. The Lincoln and Continental had unit body construction; an exterior side mirror with adjustment controls inside the car was available on the Lincoln-Continental and Cadillac; and air suspension was optional equipment on the Mercury and all General Motors cars. An off-center rear spring mounting to reduce diving when braking was offered by Studebaker-Packard. Paper air cleaners were used on a number of makes. Aluminum brake drums with cooling fins were offered on the Buick; a double compound windshield extended into the roof line on all Chrysler Corporation cars; and rear coil springs on more than half of the models. Body dip method of prime painting to reduce rust was used on the Rambler, Lincoln and Continental. A removable transistor radio on some General Motors cars was optional equipment, and a device designed to hold a car at a preselected speed for long open country trips was available on Chrysler, Imperial and Cadillac. Hardtop models were added to the Studebaker's President and Commander series; and Chevrolet added the luxury Impala series to its line of cars.

*1958* Four automotive milestones were noted during the year. Ford Motor Company produced its 50 millionth motor vehicle; Chrysler Corporation assembled its 25 millionth motor vehicle; General Motors Corporation celebrated its 50th anniversary of incorporation; and Ford Division commenorated the 50th anniversary of the Model T by reassembling a 1909 Model T at the Mahwah, New Jersey plant.

Connecticut's 129-mile turnpike opened to traffic in January, extending from Greenwich to Killingly on the Rhode Island state line.

Additions to the 1958 models included: Mercury's Medalist economy model; American Motor's 100-inch wheelbase

1958—The Thunderbird was restyled with a rear seat and unitized body construction.

Rambler American; and new four-passenger Thunderbird by Ford, with unitized body, in hardtop and convertible body styles.

An additional $1.8 billion was authorized in April to speed up construction on the Interstate Highway System.

Four-Wheel-Drive Auto Company was bought by Para-dynamics, Inc., of St. Louis, Missouri.

Ford Motor Company merged three of its car divisions into the Mercury-Edsel-Lincoln (M-E-L) Division.

White Motor Company purchased the Diamond T Motor Car Company. The wholly-owned subsidiary was renamed Diamond T Motor Truck Co.

Studebaker-Packard Corporation announced cessation of the Packard automobile, and concentration on a car with a new smaller wheelbase, the Lark.

Chrysler Corporation purchased 25 per cent of the stock of Simca, a French automotive firm.

Plans for a $17,000 hand-made car to be called the Argonaut were announced by Argonaut Motor Machine Corp., of Cleveland, Ohio.

145

1958—Chevrolet added the Impala series which featured sculptural styling.

A seven-year study by the University of Michigan to design a secondary school test for prospective students of automotive mechanics was launched by the Automobile Manufacturers Association, Inc. The study was planned to aid in selection and guidance and thus to relieve the shortage of competent mechanics.

The New York Central Railroad started a "piggy-back" service in which loaded semi-trailers were put on flat cars for rail shipment.

Goodyear Tire and Rubber Company introduced a double-chambered captive-air safety tire to avoid complete blow-outs.

At least three full size or scaled-down operating models of antique automobiles were offered for sale.

General Motors engineers demonstrated a car equipped to steer itself over a special road with wire buried in the road surface. Later in the year the firm displayed the Firebird III experimental car with a single-stick control system which eliminated the steering wheel, brake pedal, and

146

accelerator pedal. The car also had a separate power plant for accessories.

Ford Motor Company displayed a three-foot model of a Glideair vehicle which traveled on a thin cushion of air instead of wheels. A scooter version was also displayed.

The Automobile Information Disclosure Act, more commonly known as "the price label law," was passed during the summer to be effective Oct. 1. The new law required every automobile manufacturer to affix a label to the windshield or side window containing the following information: make, model and serial number, final assembly point, name and address of the dealer receiving the car, method of transport from the final assembly point to place of delivery, suggested retail price of the car, factory installed optional accessories, and transportation and delivery charges.

Checker Motors Corporation announced plans to produce the Superba passenger car.

White Motor Company started production of a Fiberglas truck cab.

Highlights and features offered in the fall for the 1959 model year included: swivel front seats as optional equipment on Chrysler Corporation cars; side view mirror controls inside the car on several makes; on Chrysler cars an electronic control which changed the rear view mirror to non-glaring automatically when a headlamp beam hit its surface; Oldsmobile offered a flanged brake drum for faster cooling; the Lark compact car was introduced by Studebaker-Packard; the Galaxie luxury series was added to the Ford line; a town car and limousine were offered in the Continental line; new body finishes that retained a luster for a greater period without waxing became standard on most passenger cars; a trunk lid catch electrically released inside the car by the driver was offered by Ford Motor Company; individually adjustable separate reclining seats were available on the Rambler; Buick renamed its line of cars—Electra (luxury), Invicta (medium) and LeSabre (lowest priced); a seat lock to prevent the back of the right front seat from suddenly moving forward was offered by Buick; and metals on tail pipe and muffler components were plated and made heavier.

*1959* During this year Pontiac Motor Division of General Motors produced its seven millionth motor vehicle.

Five experimental vehicles were displayed in 1959: De Soto had a scale model of the Cella I which featured an electrochemical system that converted liquid fuel into electrical energy to power the car; Cadillac showed its Cyclone experimental car equipped with a radar device to warn the driver of objects in the car's path; Ford Motor Company demonstrated the Levacar which floated on a cushion of air above the ground and was propelled by small jets of compressed air; Curtiss-Wright Corporation announced the development of its Air-Car, a 300-horsepower vehicle designed to travel on a cushion of low-pressure, low velocity air at a height of 6 to 12 inches; and Chevrolet displayed a heavy duty Turbo-Titan II dream truck equipped with an experimental gas turbine engine.

Three firms announced plans to manufacture electric vehicles—Nic-L-Silver Battery Company of Santa Ana, California, Stinson Aircraft and Tool Engineering Corporation of San Diego, California, and Cleveland Vehicle Company of Cleveland, Ohio.

National Standard Parts Association and the Motor and Equipment Wholesalers Association merged to form the Automotive Service Industries Association.

Chrysler Corporation announced plans to produce glass at its Detroit-area McGraw plant. The firm also realigned its car sales division by forming the Plymouth-De Soto

1959—The Imperial Southhampton hardtop had a stainless steel roof.

Division: Chrysler-Imperial Division, and the Dodge Division (cars and trucks).

Ford Motor Company established a credit and financing subsidiary, the Ford Motor Credit Company, with the first office in Indianapolis, Indiana.

Glen Alden Corporation sold its Ward LaFrance Truck Corporation division to a group of investors led by Harris J. Klein, a New York attorney. The company was a pioneer in the fire truck field.

The launching of the first mass produced Jupiter ballistic missile, made by Chrysler Corporation in Detroit, was announced by the U. S. Army.

A caravan of 16 motor vehicles with 39 men, women and children, known as the '59ers, drove from Detroit to Alaska's Susitan Valley (90 miles north of Anchorage) to homesteads in the 49th state. Marino Sik of Detroit led the pioneers over the 4,239-mile trip in 25 days.

New truck engine options offered during the year included: a diesel engine by Dodge and a V-6 diesel and V-6 and V-12 gasoline engines on GMC Truck and Coach Division vehicles.

White Motor Company purchased the Montpelier Manufacturing Company of Montpelier, Ohio, producers of small truck bodies.

Two new types of power plants were reported during the year: Curtiss-Wright Corporation and NSU Werke of West Germany announced a rotating internal combustion engine for automotive, aircraft, and marine use—the engine reportedly has only a few moving parts. Williams Research Company of Walled Lake, Michigan, reported the development of a low-cost, lightweight, medium horsepower gas turbine engine using a heat exchange principle.

Willys offered the Maverick Special—a deluxe Jeep station wagon.

Plans for the 43rd National Automobile Show to be held in Detroit's new Cobo Hall in October of 1960, were announced by the Automobile Manufacturers Association, Inc.

Federal tax on gasoline was increased from three to four cents a gallon to keep the Interstate Highway System on a "pay-as-you-go" basis.

A new seven-inch headlamp, with the approximate low beam advantages of the Dual Headlamp System, was offered for vehicles using two, instead of four, headlamps. It was developed by lamp and motor vehicle manufacturers through a committee of the Automobile Manufacturers Association.

Four new makes were offered to the motoring public for 1960. Dodge Division introduced the Dart; Chevrolet offered a light aluminum air-cooled rear engine car—the Corvair; Ford introduced the Falcon economy line; and Plymouth offered its new Valiant.

Highlighted features offered on the 1960 models included: a convertible and four-door station wagon added to the Studebaker-Packard Lark series; electroluminescent dash lighting to reduce eye strain in night driving on Chrysler Corporation cars; an alternator and rectifier a.c. generating system on the Valiant; unit body construction for Plymouth, De Soto, Dodge, Chrysler, Valiant, Corvair and Falcon; folding rear seat for luggage space on the Corvair; vacuum operated remote trunk lock control inside the car on the Oldsmobile; and vacuum safety door locks on most Chrysler cars. Also offered were: torsion bar suspension on Chevrolet trucks; a dual chambered water pump for even distribution on both cylinder banks on the V-8 Pontiac; an automatic control to turn on headlamps when driving at dusk; an air cooled torque converter transmission on the Falcon; and an adjustable mirror on the Buick to reflect the instrument panel for different heights of drivers. Other features were: a side-hinged rear station wagon door on the Rambler; self-adjusting brakes on the Cadillac; an automatic vacuum parking brake release when the transmission is put into drive position on the Cadillac; a sliding metal roof panel on Thunderbird hardtop models; an anti-theft ignition switch with three blade terminals in Ford Motor Company cars; non-round steering wheels by Chrysler; and a four-light emergency flashing system on Chrysler cars.

Ford Motor Company discontinued the Edsel line in November.

A device designed to eliminate substantial portions of smog-producing hydro-carbon emissions from automobiles would be offered on 1961 American cars produced for sale in California, the Automobile Manufacturers Association, Inc., announced on Nov. 30. The device reduced vapors from the engine crankcase by diverting them through the intake manifold.

*1960* Five new smaller, or compact automobiles were introduced during the year, bringing to 10 the total of American makes in this class. Lincoln-Mercury offered the Comet (1960 model) in March. The other four makes were 1961 models introduced in the fall—Buick's Special (aluminum V-8 engine), Oldsmobile's F-85 (aluminum V-8 engine), Pontiac's Tempest (front-mounted four-cylinder engine or a V-8 as optional equipment, and a trans-axle in the rear), and Dodge's new Lancer.

Eight automotive companies expanded their operations. American Motors added to its Kenosha and Milwaukee, Wisconsin, plants. Ford Motor Company purchased Sherman Products (manufacturers of Ford tractor accessories), and announced plans for a glass research and development center in Lincoln Park, Michigan. Chrysler Corporation dedicated a new assembly plant near St. Louis, Missouri. General Motors expanded its facilities at Warren, and at Willow Run, Michigan, and at Tarrytown, New York. Mack Trucks, Inc., announced plans to build a new plant at Hagerstown, Maryland. Studebaker-Packard Corporation acquired three firms. White Motor Company bought Oliver Corporation's farm equipment manufacturing business.

Several announcements in the experimental field were reported: General Motors' "electric fence" which would warn the driver if the vehicle was near the pavement edge, and a nuclear-powered combat vehicle for the Defense Department. Chevrolet displayed the XP-700 Corvette experimental car and Plymouth exhibited the NXR experimental sports car; Ford announced a new process for making open hearth steel that would cut production time in half.

Glen Pray of Tulsa, Oklahoma, purchased the assets of the Auburn, Cord and Duesenberg auto plant at Auburn, Indiana, and announced plans to produce parts for the three cars.

Several all-weather radiator coolants were offered by antifreeze makers.

Studies by the Automobile Manufacturers Association, Inc., showed windshield and window areas of 1960 cars provided 15 per cent greater vision for the driver compared with 1950 models. The AMA also announced grants totaling $1,706,000 to a number of organizations to promote traffic safety and efficient use of highways.

United States Freight Company offered an intercontinental piggy-back service, combining railroad, steamship and trucking methods of transport of loaded vans.

The U. S. Bureau of Public Roads reported that more than 9,100 miles of the 41,000-mile Interstate Highway System were completed, and that 4,700 additional miles were under construction.

International Harvester Co. reported it would enter the compact car field with the Scout. The new vehicle would have a four-cylinder engine and an integral body.

The National Automobile Show in Detroit's new 10-acre Cobo Hall during October officially opened the 1961 model

1960—National Auto Show, for the first time in Detroit, drew 1,403,872 visitors.

year. Sponsored by the Automobile Manufacturers Association, it was the first national show since 1956 and the first industry-sponsored show to open outside New York City. The show, with its "Wheels of Freedom" theme, set a new international record for attendance at any industrial show— nearly 1.5 million persons. More than 300 cars, trucks and motor coaches were displayed in the 300,000 square foot exhibition space. Suppliers to the automotive industry co-operated with the vehicle manufacturers to put on an "Auto Wonderland" exhibit, a 104,000 square foot display telling how a car is made. The U. S. Post Office issued a special Wheels of Freedom commemorative four-cent stamp in conjunction with the Show's opening day. President Dwight D. Eisenhower was the principal speaker at the industry's traditional banquet.

New features on the 1961 models displayed at the National Auto Show included: an economy line of trucks and station buses by Ford (Econoline) and Chevrolet Corvair; a four-door soft top convertible on the Lincoln-Continental; pre-lubrication on a number of chassis points with a special grease for 30,000 miles on Ford, Mercury and Lincoln-Continental; Cadillac featured a life-time chassis lubrication; Lark offered a sliding soft roof; aluminized mufflers and self-adjusting brakes on the Ford; ceramic-coated muffler and tail pipe on the Rambler; an aluminum six-cylinder Rambler engine; a swing-away steering wheel to assist the driver getting into or out of the Thunderbird; and two-level air conditioning to cool the top level of the car while heating the lower level for dehumidifying on the Cadillac.

Each U. S. automobile company provided embossed pads in the floor pan so dealers could make seat belt installations more easily.

New car warranties were extended by all manufacturers to at least 12 months or 12,000 miles, whichever came first.

1960—One feature of Detroit's Show was carousel of cars circling the great stage.

The Lincoln-Continental warranty was extended to 24 months or 24,000 miles.

Chrysler Corporation announced it would discontinue the De Soto at the end of November.

Two rebate plans were disclosed. Studebaker-Packard offered shareholders a refund of $100 for buying a Studebaker car or truck during a three-month period. American Motors Corporation offered U. S. savings bonds as rebates to purchasers of its cars during a four-month period, providing the firm's car sales rose 10 per cent above the same period in the previous year.

*1961* Chevrolet Motor Division produced its 44-millionth vehicle.

Five experimental vehicles were exhibited during the year. Chrysler Corporation displayed its Turboflite and X7, both powered by a gas turbine engine. Ford Motor Company exhibited the two-wheeled gyroscope-controlled Gyron. Dodge Division's Fleetwing went on display in New York. Ford Motor Company unveiled a scale model of a 200-passenger Levacar, called the Aerolus. The vehicle slides on a film of air a fraction of an inch above special rail surfaces.

New mid-year models introduced by the industry included: Cadillac Division's Town Sedan in the Calais series; Oldsmobile Division's Starfire sports convertible, a three-seat station wagon in the F-85 series, the F-85 Cutlass and F-85 economy club coupe; Chrysler Corporation's Enforcer, a new model especially equipped for police work, and the Hylander in the Newport series; American Motors' Custom 400 Series in the Rambler American, Classic and Ambassador V-8 lines; Ford Division's Futura in the Falcon line; Dodge Division's 770 Lancer sports coupe; and Buick Division's Skylark, a top-of-the-line model in the Special series.

New models offered in the fall for the 1962 model year included: Chevrolet's new Chevy II series; Mercury's Meteor series; Pontiac's Gran Prix series, Studebaker-Packard's Gran Turismo in the Hawk series; and Chrysler's 300-H, a high performance sports-type car.

Numerous product innovations were introduced with the 1962 models. Dual-brake systems became standard equipment on all 1962 American Motors and Cadillac models. American Motors announced it would offer factory-installed seat belts on all Ramblers for both front and rear seats. American Motors also introduced the E-stick automatic clutch transmission on its Rambler American series. The driver shifts gears manually, but the clutch is automatically engaged and disengaged.

Ford Motor Company introduced a clutch interlock for manual transmissions that prevented shifting into low or reverse by mistake.

Single-leaf rear-spring suspension systems were offered on the Chevy II. Dodge Dart, Phoenix, and Pioneer models

1961—Restyled Falcon featured a convex-shaped aluminum grille.

1961—The extra space in the passenger compartment and trunk introduced a pleasant luxury to the Dodge Lancer.

157

adopted dual tail lights as standard equipment. Ford Motor Company offered an engine coolant said to be good for 30,000 miles or two years of driving.

New models and product innovations in the trucking industry included: International Harvester's new line of all-purpose vehicles, including the Scout which can be converted from an enclosed runabout, small pickup or panel truck, to an open model without top, windows or doors. Other models offered were the Travelall, a nine-passenger four-door station wagon, and the Travelette, a four-door, six-passenger pickup truck. General Motors developed the first production models of a new line of inter-city coaches powered by V-8 diesel engines. Willys Motors, Inc., introduced its new Jeep Fleetvan, a half-ton walk-in delivery vehicle.

Studebaker-Packard Corporation announced it would produce a line of medium-duty trucks and truck tractors with diesel engines.

The Detroit Diesel Engine Division of General Motors unveiled a group of 12 engines which can run on a complete range of fuels from gasoline to diesel fuel. In addition, the division developed conversion kits which can change present diesel engines into multi-fuel engines.

Ford Motor Company purchased the Philco Corporation and two Electric Autolite Company plants. Studebaker-Packard purchased Chemical Compounds, Inc., makers of STP, a motor-oil additive, and bought Curtiss-Wright Corporation's South Bend plant. American Motors opened a new engineering and research unit in Kenosha, Wisconsin. Chrysler Corporation combined the marketing operations of its Chrysler-Imperial Division and Plymouth Division into a single Chrysler-Plymouth Division. Oldsmobile Division dedicated a new engineering center.

Most major tire producers developed two-ply tires as a replacement for four-ply on compact cars. Goodyear Tire and Rubber Co. announced production of Budene, a new synthetic rubber expected to nearly double the life of tires.

Chrysler Corporation engineers drove a turbine-powered Dodge Dart from New York to Los Angeles for an engineering evaluation run.

Secretary of Commerce Luther H. Hodges announced the official start of the National Driver Register Service. The Service cross-indexes data on motorists in 43 states whose licenses have been revoked on charges of drunken driving or highway-death cases.

*1962* General Motors produced its 75,000,000th car, a Bonneville convertible, made by Pontiac Division. Ford Motor Company became the first automobile manu-

1962—The Studebaker Gran Turismo Hawk incorporated a low silhouette, flat roof line and long tapering hood.

facturer to reach the 30 million mark in production of V-8 engines.

Studebaker dropped the Packard name from its corporate title.

Amber lights for front turn signals were adopted by the entire industry after a recommendation by the AMA Board of Directors. Extensive visibility tests proved that amber signals are seen more readily against glaring reflections than white signals.

Shelby American, Inc., a Los Angeles-based firm, began producing a high-performance sports car called the Cobra. The car was powered by a Ford V-8 engine, the chassis and aluminum body were made in England.

Thirteen mid-year makes were introduced: Buick's new sports models, the Wildcat hardtop and the Skylark convertible; Checker Motors Corporation's new station wagon, the Aerobus, available in 9- or 12-passenger models; Chevrolet's Corvair Monza convertible and Monza Spyder; Dodge's Custom 880; Ford's Galaxy 500XL, Fairlane Sports Coupe and Falcon Sports Futura; Lincoln-Mercury's Villager, a compact station wagon; Oldsmobile's Jetfire sports coupe, the first American production car equipped with a fluid injected turbo-charged V-8 engine; Plymouth's Sports Fury; and Studebaker's new sports coupe, the Avanti.

New models introduced in the fall included: Pontiac's LeMans in the Tempest series; Buick's Riviera; Checker's station wagon, the Texan; Chrysler's two-door hardtop model, the 300-J; and Studebaker's new Lark Standard series, aimed at the fleet buyer.

The tire and rubber industry announced several new developments. A new tire cord made of polyester fiber that combined the best features of nylon and rayon was developed by Goodyear Tire and Rubber Company. A tire introduced by the General Tire and Rubber Company was

1962—Simulated wood paneling distinguished the styling of the Mercury Comet Villager.

claimed to last 50,000 miles or more. A new chemical bonding agent that solved the problem of ply and tread separation was introduced by U. S. Rubber.

Numerous new features and product innovations were introduced on new model cars. Studebaker's 1963s featured front-wheel disc brakes as an option, and as standard equipment on the Avanti. Self-adjusting brakes were installed on most 1963 models. All models were provided with seat-belt anchors for the front seat. Pontiac offered a fully transistorized ignition system as an option on its 1963 models.

The industry started nationwide installation of positive crankcase ventilating systems on all 1963 model cars and light trucks.

Developments in the gas turbine-engine field continued. To test consumer acceptance, Chrysler Corporation started building 50 turbine-powered passenger cars for distribution to selected motorists in the latter part of 1963. Dodge Truck Division displayed an experimental turbine-powered truck. Ford Motor Company tested an experimental turbine-engine in a 1955 Thunderbird.

New experimental cars exhibited during the year included: Ford's Cougar 406, a sports model featuring electrically operated gull-wing doors; Chevrolet's Cerv-I; Pontiac's Monte Carlo, a two-passenger luxury model featuring magnesium wheels; and American Motors' Metropolitan Royal Runabout.

Continental Motors produced a new multi-fuel engine for the Army, called the Hypercycle LDS-427-2.

Manufacturers offered an expanded selection of mobile homes and campers, a result of the continued rise and popularity of camping as a family recreation. The Champ, a many-purpose camper, was introduced by Studebaker. Special motor-home bodies were available for Chevrolet, Dodge, and Ford truck chassis. Ford Division announced the availability of the Condor, a complete self-contained unit built on a modified Ford truck chassis. Traville Corporation of Detroit produced a self-powered deluxe travel home called the Traville, mounted on a one-ton Chevrolet chassis.

The 44th National Automobile Show was visited by 1,147,742 persons during its nine-day run in Detroit's Cobo Hall.

A scaled-down version of the famed Cord 810, the Sportsman, was announced by Glenn Pray of Oklahoma for limited production.

The International Rectifier Company unveiled a solar energy-propelled Baker electric (1912 vintage) car. The vehicle was outfitted with a roof deck composed of 10,640 individual solar cells.

American Motors opened an Eastern Division Parts Warehouse in Philadelphia and announced a major expansion program at its Kelvinator plant in Grand Rapids, Michigan. Ford Motor Company completed a major expansion program at its Metuchen, New Jersey, plant. General Motors erected new buildings or additions at its plant in Warren, Michigan, at its Saginaw Steering Gear Division Plant, and at its Cadillac Division Detroit plant. Chrysler Corporation purchased a plant in Warren, Michigan, for the construction of mobile airport lounges. Studebaker Corporation acquired Paxton Products, Inc., a maker of superchargers for automobiles and other vehicles, and also purchased the Franklin Manufacturing Company, a Minneapolis manufacturer of refrigerators and other appliances.

Six new truck models were introduced during the year. General Motors displayed its 6500 series featuring a V-6 gasoline engine. White Motor introduced a new line of trucks, the White 7000 series. International Harvester brought its Loadstar Line, a series of medium and light-heavy duty trucks. Mack Trucks introduced its F series featuring diesel or gasoline engines anc four- and six-wheel chassis options. Willys Motors displayed a new series of four-wheel-drive trucks named the Gladiator line.

Studebaker featured a shorter diesel truck tractor in its E-45 line, permitting the tractor to be combined with a 40-foot trailer and still meet the legal length requirements of states.

# 1963
Studebaker halted production of automobiles in the United States on December 20. While continuing to sell cars in the U. S., the company moved its primary base of automotive manufacturing to Hamilton, Ontario.

The Marmon-Herrington Company, after 31 years in operation, announced it would leave the automotive business.

1963—An engineering and consumer evaluation program was launched by Chrysler Corporation with its specially designed turbine car.

Kaiser JEEP Corporation, formerly Willys Motors, Inc., moved its headquarters from Toledo, Ohio, to Oakland, California. The Automotive Division of the corporation maintained its executive offices and operations in Toledo.

Two production milestones were established during the year. Ford Motor Company produced its 60-millionth vehicle, and Chevrolet Division produced its 50-millionth vehicle.

New 1963 models introduced included: Chrysler's new luxury model, the New Yorker Salon; Lincoln-Mercury's Comet Sportster and the Marauder in its regular series; and Studebaker's Super-Lark and Super-Hawk.

Checker Motor Corporation revealed technical details of a new Town Custom limousine scheduled for limited production.

Five new 1964 models were introduced in the fall of the year. Chevrolet brought out a new line of cars called the

Chevelle. Oldsmobile introduced its new Jetstar 88 series and a new sports-type car, the Jetstar I. Studebaker unveiled its new model, the Challenger. Lincoln-Mercury added the Caliente series to its Comet line.

Lincoln-Mercury dropped its Meteor line at the end of the 1963 model run.

Experimental vehicles with internal combustion engines and turbine-power plants were exhibited during the year. Chrysler Corporation introduced a new turbine engine in a specially styled Chrysler turbine car. Ford Motor Company began testing a 300-HP turbine engine in an experimental truck. Pontiac introduced the X-400. Oldsmobile exhibited the J-TR, a four-passenger convertible. Plymouth unveiled its experimental convertible, the Satellite. The Monza GT and Monza SS were exhibited by Chevrolet. Ford Motor Company unveiled the Allegro, Cougar II, and Mustang II.

1963—The highly stylized Buick Riviera was introduced in the fall of 1962 as a two-door hardtop.

Lincoln-Mercury introduced the Super Cyclone, Mercury Montego and Super Marauder.

Major construction completed at existing plant sites during the year included: General Motors' expansion and modernization of its Tarrytown, New York, Chevrolet and Fisher Body assembly plants; Ford Motor Company's expansion of its assembly facilities at the Rouge plant in Dearborn, Michigan; and completion of a new final assembly line at American Motors' Kenosha, Wisconsin, assembly plant.

International Harvester acquired an assembly plant in San Leandro, California, from the Kaiser Aluminum & Chemical Corporation, for the production of heavy-duty trucks.

Studebaker Corporation, following a policy of making running rather than annual model changes, began installing seat belts during March. Front-seat belts were installed as standard equipment on all other cars beginning with the 1964 model run. Other innovations developed during the year included: Push-button operated headlights that swing out of the fender's forward edges were offered on the Chevrolet Corvette, and Cadillac Motor Division's Twilight Sentinel, an option that automatically turns headlights on at dusk or off at dawn when the ignition switch is on.

Highlights and features of the trucking industry during 1963 included: The American Association of State Highway Officials recommended that maximum gross weights of truck combinations be increased from 73,280 pounds to between 88,000 and 90,000 pounds, maximum width be increased from 96 to 102 inches and height from 12½ to 13½ feet, and permissible length of single units increased from 35 to 40 feet. International Harvester introduced a new light-duty truck, the model 900, and a new 210 series of heavy-duty trucks. Studebaker's new "Service Champ" was announced as America's first 1/2 and 3/4-ton service truck bodies of reinforced fiberglass. Chevrolet Division announced it would start production in late 1963 of a light-duty panel delivery van, the Chevy Van.

Three new mobile homes were introduced during the year. International Harvester unveiled a family camper adaptation of its Scout utility vehicle. Clark Equipment Company introduced the Cortez, a mobile home that provided living and sleeping facilities for four adults. Stewart Coach Industries, of Bristol, Indiana, offered a 17-foot trailer that could also be converted into a home on water.

Goodyear Tire & Rubber Company introduced a premium safety tire featuring an inner "spare" on which a motorist can continue to drive for 100 miles or more after the outer carcass blows.

*1964* Four automotive milestones were passed during the year. General Motors Corporation, with its five divisions, produced more than four million vehicles in the 1964 model year, the first time any manufacturer had done so. For the first time new car registrations went over the eight million mark. Dodge Division celebrated its 50th year in the automotive industry. Studebaker Corporation stopped producing engines with the closedown of its South Bend, Indiana, plant. The company began using engines produced by General Motors.

Three new sports-type cars appeared during mid-1964. Ford introduced the Mustang, Chrysler-Plymouth unveiled the Barracuda and American Motors brought out the Marlin.

New models introduced in the fall for the 1965 model run included: Chrysler-Plymouth's 300-L; Dodge's new intermediate Coronet series, and the Dodge Monaco, a top of the line two-door hardtop; Ford's LTD in the Galaxie series; and Buick's Gran Sports models of the Skylark and Riviera series.

Fritz Duesenberg, son of one of the brothers who produced Duesenbergs in the 1920s and 1930s, announced that a new firm had been founded in Indianapolis to build modern luxury cars patterned after the famous old Duesenberg.

The selector pattern of automatic transmissions was standardized as Park-Reverse-Neutral-Drive-Low. Manufacturers began switching to anti-glare suede paint for dashboards. They also offered disc brakes on many 1965 models. Ford applied paint primer by a new process called electrocoating on '64 Thunderbirds and Lincolns.

American Motors, Ford and General Motors adopted a two-year or 24,000-mile warranty, whichever came first, on all parts except tires, which are warranted by the tire manufacturer. Chrysler Corporation offered a five-year or 50,000-mile warranty on the engine, transmission, driveline and rear axle.

New plants and expansion programs completed by manufacturers included: General Motors' Fremont, California, assembly plant; Cadillac Division's expansion program at its Detroit facilities, including the dedication of a new engineering center; Ford Motor Company's expansion and conversion of its Nashville, Tennessee, factory to the manufacturing of float glass, and the completion of its new steel making facilities at its Rouge plant in Dearborn, Michigan; and American Motor's new engine and axle plant in Kenosha, Wisconsin.

New developments in the trucking industry included the introduction of Dodge's new Camper Wagon; GMC Truck and Coach Division's Handi-Van, a light duty truck; and Kaiser JEEP Corporation's Tuxedo Park IV, a sporty version of its Jeep Universal. GMC Truck and Bus Division introduced two forged I-Beam axles for front-wheel suspensions of light trucks.

New experimental vehicles exhibited during the year

1964—The Ford Mustang featured a long hood and short deck with its sports-car styling.

1964—The fast-back styling of the Plymouth Barracuda included a smooth contour line made by the roof, rear window and rear deck.

169

included: Lincoln-Mercury's Park Lane 400, featuring electric blanket-type heating elements installed in the seats; General Motors' Firebird IV, Runabout and GM-X; Chevrolet's Toronado and Chevy II Super Nova. Other vehicles shown included: Buick's Silver Arrow; American Motors' Rambler Tarpon; Dodge's Charger II; and Ford's experimental station wagon, the Aurora.

Developments in the gas turbine field continued as Ford Motor Company introduced a 600 HP truck tractor. General Motors displayed its Turbo Cruiser No. 2, a turbine-powered bus and a turbine-powered freight hauler, called the Bison, designed especially to carry containerized cargo. Chrysler Corporation continued its public testing program of its turbine car.

*1965* Passenger-car and commercial-vehicle production in 1965 established all-time records. Automobile production totaled 9,335,277 units, almost 1.4 million above the previous peak established in 1955. Truck and bus production climbed to 1,802,603 units, more than 240 thousand vehicles above the previous high established in 1964.

The United States and Canada agreed to eliminate tariffs on new motor vehicles and original parts for production of new vehicles. The agreement was known as the Automotive Products Trade Act of 1965.

The U. S. motor-vehicle industry granted $10 million to the University of Michigan to establish a highway-research institute and to aid in its support for the first five years. The grant was described by university officials as the largest corporate gift ever received by a university for any purpose.

Chevrolet Division of General Motors became the first producer in the industry to build more than three million cars and trucks in a single year.

A program to establish a nationwide communications network to aid motorists in distress was announced by

1965—Fender skirts and stainless steel on the lower body were two styling highlights of the 1965 Pontiac Bonneville.

the Automobile Manufactuers Association. The system, known as HELP for Highway Emergency Locating Plan, called for the use of Citizens Band two-way radio equipment in private passenger cars. Motorists in need of aid would make their needs known on CB Channel Nine where the message could be picked up by a round-the-clock monitoring station within the 10-to-20-mile range of the equipment.

Experimental vehicles displayed during the year included: American Motors' St. Maritz and the Tahiti; Plymouth's XP-Vip; Lincoln-Mercury's Mercury Astron, Comet Escapade, Comet Cyclone Sportster and Lincoln Continental Coronation Coupe; Dodge's Charger II; Ford's Bordinet Cobra, Mercer Cobra, GT Mark I and the Black Pearl; and Chevrolet's Mako-Shark II and Concours.

Chevrolet Division unveiled its truck of tomorrow with its tractor powered by a 280 HP gas turbine engine.

As part of its truck-turbine program, Ford Motor Company tested its 600 HP turbine truck on a cross country tour. Chrysler Corporation completed its two-year turbine consumer-research testing program.

Rear seat belts became standard equipment on all 1966

models. Dual braking systems were made available on all 1967 U. S.-produced cars. Pontiac introduced an overhead camshaft six-cylinder engine standard on all Tempest, Tempest Custom and LeMans models for 1966. All Ford station wagons featured a dual tailgate that opens either as a tailgate for loading cargo or sideways as a conventional passenger car door.

American Motors Corporation dropped the "Rambler" prefix on its Ambassador line.

The Avanti II, a car similar in design to the Avanti formerly made by Studebaker Corporation, was introduced in August. Made by the Avanti Motor Corporation, South Bend, Indiana, the new Avanti had a fiberglass body and was powered by a Chevrolet engine.

The Cord Automobile Company of Oklahoma began production of the scaled-down model of the classic Cord of the 1930's called the Sportsman.

1965—Dodge's new intermediate Coronet line of cars included the Coronet 440 four-door sedan.

Chevrolet Division introduced the Sportsvan, a vehicle built with a commercial chassis but including passenger car equipment.

Oldsmobile Division introduced its 1966 Toronado, the first car with front-wheel drive to be built in the United States since 1937. Other new models offered during the fall included: Chrysler-Plymouth Division's Town and Country Station Wagon in the Chrysler Newport series and the Plymouth Vip in the Fury line; American Motors' three new top of the line models, the DPL in the Ambassador line, Rebel in the Classic line and the Rogue in the American line; Ford Motor Company introduced the Bronco, a four-wheeled drive jeep-type vehicle, and added the Fairlane 500/XL and Fairlane GT as new models to its existing line; Chevrolet Division introduced the Caprice, a top of the line model in its Impala series; Lincoln-Mercury Division added the Capri to its Mercury Comet series; Dodge Division introduced its new sports fastback, the Charger; and Shelby American, Inc., introduced the Shelby GT 350, a modified high performance version of the Ford Mustang Fastback.

Highway Products, Inc., of Ohio offered a new line of trucks, called Compac-Vans. Powered by Cummings, Ford, General Motors or Chrysler engines, the units are of an integrated design so that the entire truck including cab, floor, roof and fluted aluminum sides are constructed as a single unit.

Chrysler Corporation announced that it had purchased the Lone Star Boat Company of Plano, Texas.

Major construction of manufacturing facilities completed in 1965 included: Ford Motor Company's Woodhaven, Michigan, stamping plant; Chrysler Corporation's Belvidere, Illinois, assembly plant and its stamping plant in Sterling Township, Michigan. General Motors dedicated its new training center in Detroit.

1966—The Vixen, an American Motors experimental car, featured a landau-type roof with canted vents in the rear.

*1966* The year was highlighted by enactment of the National Traffic and Motor Vehicle Safety Act and the Highway Safety Act and establishment of the Department of Transportation.

The National Traffic and Motor Vehicle Safety Act was designed to provide and coordinate a national safety program and establish safety standards for motor vehicles. The Highway Safety Act sought to establish a coordinated national highway safety program through financial assistance to the states to accelerate highway-traffic safety programs. The Department of Transportation was formed to insure that the general welfare and the economic growth and stability of the nation would benefit from policies that would enable fast, safe, efficient and convenient transportation at the lowest cost consistent with other national objectives.

After 64 years as an automobile manufacturer, Studebaker Corporation in Canada terminated car production

174

in March. The first Studebaker, an electric vehicle, was built in 1902. The corporation ended production in the United States in December 1963.

New interest in electric vehicles was aroused as two major motor-vehicle manufacturers outlined their research and testing programs for electric cars. General Motors demonstrated two electric vehicles, a fuel-cell van called the Electrovan and battery-powered Corvair, the Electrovair II. Ford Motor Company announced the development of a new sealed sodium-sulphur battery for electrical vehicles designed to last the life of the vehicle.

1966—The distinctive Oldsmobile Toronado featured front-wheel drive.

Collapsible steering columns were installed on all General Motors, Chrysler Corporation, and American Motors cars. Ford Motor Company offered a newly designed energy-absorbing steering wheel featuring a padded hub. Oldsmobile Division offered as an option an engine pre-

175

heater designed to keep carburetor inlet temperatures at about 100 degrees, allowing easier cold-weather starting. Optional on 400- and 425-cubic-inch V-8 Oldsmobile engines was an ultra-high-voltage capacitor system. The new system fires fouled plugs to boost their life nearly four times and eliminates engine ignition tuneup for at least 24,000 miles. General Motors, Ford, and American Motors followed Chrysler Corporation in adopting the five-year or 50,000-mile warranty on the engine, transmission, driveline, and rear axle. Chrysler extended its total car warranty to 24 months or 24,000 miles. All 1967 cars had underbodies made of corrosion-resistant galvanized steel for added anti-rust protection.

Two new sports-type cars were introduced during the fall of the year. Lincoln-Mercury Division brought out its Cougar and Chevrolet Division introduced its Camaro. Other new models offered included Chevrolet's Concourse, an addition to the Chevelle series; Dodge's two additions to its Coronet series, the Coronet SE and R/T; Kaiser JEEP Corporation's Super Wagoneer, a luxury station wagon available in 2- or 4-wheel drive; Lincoln-Mercury's new series, the Mercury-Marquis and Mercury Brougham; Cadillac's five-passenger Fleetwood Eldorado; and the Shelby GT 500 by Shelby American, Inc.

Production of the Sportsman, a smaller model of the Classic Cord, terminated in July. Less than 100 of the vehicles had been built when the company was placed in receivership.

Five idea cars were exhibited during the year to test consumer reaction. American Motors displayed Cavalier, Vixen, AMX and AMX II, and Pontiac introduced its Banshee.

White Motor Company developed a heavy-duty truck engine which combines the advantages of both diesel and gasoline in a power plant using regular gasoline and weighing 40 per cent less than a diesel engine. Dodge Division offered an automatic dock leveler, a Hi-Lo hydraulic body lift mounted on a Dodge W-500 four wheel drive truck. The unit can be raised from ground level to 48 inches. White Truck's new 4000 and 9000 model series of heavy duty trucks featured fiberglass frame-mounted fenders easily removed for full engine accessibility with a fiberglass integral hood and fender assembly optional. International Harvester exhibited a Scout 800 with Dreamer camper insert and a D-1000 Travelall with compact trailer. Minibus, Inc., began supplying 19–23 passenger miniature buses to metropolitan areas for short-haul downtown service.

White Motor Company announced purchase of Hercules Engine Division of the Hupp Corporation.

New facilities completed during the year included: Chrysler Corporation's truck assembly plant in Fenton, Missouri, and the Huber Avenue Foundry in Detroit; Mack Truck Corporation's Product Development Center in Allentown, Pennsylvania; International Harvester Corporation's Springfield, Ohio, assembly plant; General Motors' new Chevrolet and Fisher Body assembly plants at Lordstown, Ohio, and its Central Foundry Division's new iron foundry at Defiance, Ohio; Ford Motor Company's automotive safety research center in Dearborn, Michigan; and American Motors completion of a major expansion program at its proving ground near Burlington, Wisconsin.

1967—The five-passenger Fleetwood Eldorado combined front-wheel drive, variable ratio-power steering and automatic level control for luxury driving.

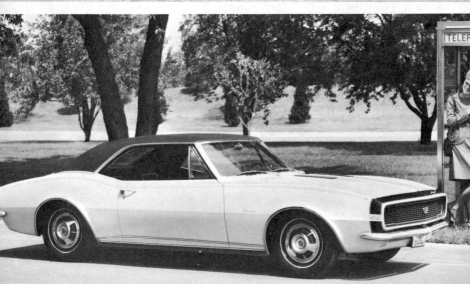

1967—A wide "bumble bee" paint band on the nose helped distinguish Chevrolet's Camaro.

# pioneers

In the 19th century, the nearest thing to a practical form of personalized transportation was the horse and buggy. But there were men in America who envisioned something better. It was the imagination, resourcefulness and determination of men such as these that brought to America three million miles of modern roads and streets traveled by more than 70 million cars, trucks and buses.

## APPERSON, Edgar

**1870•1959** On July 4, 1894, drove his first car, manufactured on assignment for Elwood Haynes, with whom he and his brother Elmer later formed Haynes-Apperson Auto Company . . . after dissolution of Haynes-Apperson, Edgar and his brother formed Apperson Brothers Motor Car Company to manufacture the Apperson *Jack Rabbit* . . . following his brother's death, Edgar sold to a syndicate in 1924 . . . in 1946 made the initial member of industry's "Hall of Fame."

## APPERSON, Elmer

**1861•1920** Collaborated with brother Edgar on the manufacture of Elwood Haynes' first car . . . partner in both the Haynes-Apperson and the Apperson Brothers Motor Car

Company . . . died while watching auto race at Los Angeles Speedway.

## BENDIX, Vincent

**1883●1945** In 1907 organized an auto firm, and sold some 7,000 Bendix motor buggies before the company failed . . . developed the starter drive which bears his name, first selling it to the Eclipse Machine Company in 1913 . . . became a leader in the aircraft field, and sponsor of the Bendix-Transcontinental Air Races.

## BRISCOE, Benjamin

**1869●1945** Founded the Briscoe Manufacturing Company in 1887 . . . in 1903 joined with Jonathan Maxwell to form the Maxwell-Briscoe Motor Company . . . in 1910 organized the United States Motor Company, a short-lived (1912) aggregation of some 130 separate firms . . . left United States Motor Company in 1912, and in 1913 organized the Briscoe Motor Company and the Argo Motor Company to manufacture cyclecars.

## BRISCOE, Frank

**1875●1954** Founder and president of Brush Runabout Company . . . also connected with brother Benjamin with Briscoe Manufacturing Company . . . other endeavors included interests in Maxwell-Briscoe, United States Motor Company, and Briscoe Motor Company.

## BUICK, David Dunbar

**1855●1929** Instrumental in devising a technique for applying enamel to cast iron . . . using the money he received from his plumbing ventures, Buick in 1902 founded the Buick Manufacturing Company to work on a valve-in-head engine . . . having perfected the engine, he organized Buick Motor Car Company in 1903 with the backing of the Briscoe brothers . . . the company was unsuccessful, and on Nov. 1, 1904, William Durant bought the controlling interest.

## CHALMERS, Hugh

**1873•1932** Worked for National Cash Register from the time he was 14, rose to vice president before he was 30 . . . in 1907 bought the Thomas half of the Thomas-Detroit Company . . . by 1909 had complete control of Chalmers Detroit, then renamed the Chalmers Motor Company . . . Chalmers backed Harry W. Ford's Saxon Motor Company in 1913 in a spectacular, though eventually unsuccessful, attempt to challenge the Model T . . . became chairman of the board of Chalmers when it was leased to Maxwell in 1917, a position he held until his retirement in 1922.

## CHAPIN, Roy D.

**1880•1936** First worked for Ransom E. Olds as a photographer and gear filer . . . while still in Olds' employ, drove a 1901 curved-dash model to New York for the second annual National Auto Show . . . left Olds in 1906 to organize, along with Howard E. Coffin, Thomas-Detroit Company later Chalmers-Detroit Company . . . in 1909, again with H. E. Coffin, Chapin with the backing of J. L. Hudson left Chalmers-Detroit to organize and head Hudson Motor Car Company . . . backed movement for good roads as chairman of numerous highway institutions . . . served as Secretary of Commerce under President Herbert Hoover in 1932.

## CHEVROLET, Louis

**1878●1941**  Came to the United States from Switzerland in 1900 to sell a wine pump which he had invented . . . drove with brothers Gaston and Arthur . . . raced against Barney Oldfield . . . his racing style attracted William C. Durant, who engaged Chevrolet as team driver for Buick . . . designed the first models of the Chevrolet for the Chevrolet Motor Car Company in 1911 . . . president of Frontenac Motor Company, which, in addition to race cars, made a racing conversion for the Model T Ford.

## CHRYSLER, Walter P.

**1875●1940**  Left his job as works manager for American Locomotive in 1911 to join Buick Motor Company . . . when he left General Motors for Willys in 1920, Chrysler was president of Buick and first vice president of General Motors . . . at Willys Chrysler was executive vice-president engaged primarily in saving the company from bankruptcy . . . almost simultaneously, he was attempting to salvage the foundering Maxwell-Chalmers Company . . . by 1922 Willys was back on its feet, and Chrysler turned his full attention to the Maxwell-Chalmers situation . . . in 1924 he brought Maxwell-Chalmers out of the woods with the introduction at the National Automobile Show of the new Chrysler models . . . shortly thereafter, Chase Securities Corporation agreed to lend Maxwell $50 million, and the corporation that was to become Chrysler was on its way . . . the years following 1924 brought continuing success to the Chrysler Corporation.

## CLIFTON, Colonel Charles

**1853●1928**  In 1897 left Ball, Lewis and Yates Coal Mining Company to become secretary and treasurer for George N.

Pierce Company . . . remained treasurer after a 1909 reorganization which saw the formation of Pierce-Arrow Motor Car Company . . . in 1916, Colonel Clifton became president of Pierce-Arrow, and in 1919 was named chairman of its board of directors . . . apart from his duties with Pierce-Arrow, Colonel Clifton served as president of National Automobile Chamber of Commerce from its birth in 1913 until March 2, 1927, when he resigned his active post to serve in an honorary capacity.

### DOBLE, Abner

**1890•1961** Built his first steam car at the age of 16, and in his spare time as a student at MIT he designed and built several more . . . in 1914 he drove a prototype model to Detroit where he found recognition and backing . . . four years later 80 Doble Detroit Steam cars had been built . . . in 1920 he founded Doble Steam Motors in the San Francisco area . . . much of Doble's fame came as a result of the prominence of his clientele . . . Hollywood stars and starlets of the day along with royalty from Europe and Asia absorbed much of his modest production . . . in later years Doble spent much of his time abroad working as a steam power consultant to locomotive manufacturers and other firms . . . he returned to the U.S. in 1950 . . . ill health forced him into retirement in the early 1950's.

### DODGE BROTHERS, John and Horace

John **1864•1920**, Horace **1868•1920** After working as machinists for several companies, the brothers developed a ball bearing bicycle and organized Evans and Dodge Bicycle Company to manufacture it . . . after numerous financial transactions, their company was absorbed by a Canadian firm and the Dodges went to Detroit to open a machine shop . . . in 1901 and 1902 they made transmissions for the Olds Motor Works . . . in 1903 Henry Ford offered each of the brothers 50 shares of stock in his new company, provided they would manufacture engines for him . . . although criticized by friends for doing so, the Dodges accepted Ford's terms, becoming the owners of one-tenth of the newly formed Ford Motor Company . . . in 1919 they received $25,000,000 for their original $20,000 investment . . . the Dodge Brothers left Ford to found their own company, Dodge Brothers, Inc., and manufactured their Dodge Brothers car.

## DUESENBERG, Frederick Samuel

**1877•1932** By 1902 Duesenberg's racing experience had won him a position as test driver for the Rambler Company . . . in 1904 he designed his own car, a racer, which was manufactured by the Mason Auto Company until 1910 . . . about that time, Duesenberg designed his famous horizontal valve engines and introduced them to the racing world . . . in 1913 the Duesenberg Motor Company was organized, producing a multitude of engines for the war effort . . . following the war, Fred and brother August organized Duesenberg Brothers Incorporated to manufacture the racing machines which in 1919 captured all the world's records up to 300 miles in every class from 161 to 450 cubic inches . . . although E. L. Cord bought control of his company in 1927, Duesenberg remained active in racing until his death, the result of a driving accident.

## DURANT, William Crapo

**1860•1947** At 25, Durant teamed with Dallas Dort to form the Durant-Dort Carriage Company, manufacturers of two-wheeled carts . . . in 1904 Durant bought out and reorganized Buick Motor Car Company . . . after a 1908 attempt to merge Buick, Maxwell-Briscoe, Ford, and Reo proved unsuccessful, Durant on Sept. 16, 1908, launched the General Motors Co. . . . in the next two years, Durant bought in quick succession Cadillac, Olds, Oakland, Carter, Elmore, Ewing, Welch and several other lesser auto producers . . . financial difficulties forced Durant out of General Motors in 1910, but by 1915, after his spectacular success with Chevrolet, "Fabulous Billy" was back to take over the corporation he had founded . . . Durant remained at the head of GM until 1920, when a depression saw the corporation's stock tumble from $400 to $12 a share despite his attempts to turn the tide . . . 1920 saw a management reorganization at General Motors leaving Durant on his own to start over again . . . ane start he did, participating in a series of enterprises ranging from Durant, Dort, and Star cars to Flint cars and finally Mason trucks . . . the 1929 depression, however, all but ended Durant's financial undertakings, and he lived in comparative obscurity until his death.

## DURYEA, Charles E.

**1861•1939** Started in the bicycle business . . . by 1891 had secured financial backing for a carriage-engine combination of his own design . . . September 22, 1893, was recorded in the Springfield "Evening Union" as the official debut of the first Duryea car, whose creation is still lost in controversy between Charles E. and brother J. Frank . . . after proving the vehicle's reliability in numerous races, the brothers went into business as the Duryea Motor Wagon Company in 1896 . . . two years later both Duryeas left the company, and Charles E. organized the Duryea Power Company of Reading, Pennsylvania, which manufactured a three-cylinder car until 1914 . . . after 1914 Duryea devoted much of his time to the writing of textbooks about the automobile.

### ERSKINE, Albert Russel

**1871•1933**  Became treasurer of Studebaker in 1910 . . . became first vice president in 1913, and president in 1915 . . . in 1928, as president, Erskine witnessed the greatest sales in the company's history up to that time . . . in that same year, he negotiated the Pierce-Arrow-Studebaker merger.

### FISHER BROTHERS, Frederic J., Charles T., Alfred J., Lawrence P., Howard A.

Frederic **1878•1941**, Charles **1880•1963**, Alfred **1892• 1963**, Lawrence **1888•1961**, Howard **1902•1942**  With skills acquired from their father, a master carriage maker, and $50,000 in capital, Frederic and Charles established the Fisher Body Company in 1908, and in succeeding years Lawrence, Alfred and Howard were brought into the business . . . Frederic and Charles realized that motoring would remain a seasonal activity until motorists could be protected from the elements . . . they began campaigning for closed bodies, and in 1910 their efforts were rewarded when 150 closed bodies were ordered by the Cadillac Motor Company . . . in December of that year the Fisher Closed Body Company was formed . . . in 1916 the two companies were merged into the Fisher Body Corporation . . . the brothers sold their corporation to General Motors, their biggest customer, in 1926 for an estimated $208 million of General Motors stock . . . the brothers became key General Motors officials, helping to run the firm's newly acquired Fisher Body Division . . . Lawrence became president of the Cadillac Motor Car Company one of General Motors' biggest divisions . . . Frederic and Charles, both GM vice-presidents, retired in 1934 to devote their time to personal business interests and philanthropic organizations . . .

## FORD, Henry

**1863•1947** As a youngster Ford showed his mechanical aptitude by constructing a steam engine when he was 15, and became an expert watch repairman before he was twenty . . . his first car, built while he was an engineer with the Edison Illuminating Company, made its first successful run in 1896 . . . in 1899 he resigned from Edison to become chief engineer for the Detroit Automobile Company, remaining with them until 1902 . . . in that year, Ford left Detroit Automobile (later reorganized as the Henry Ford Company, and finally the Cadillac Automobile Company) because of policy differences . . . six months later he organized Ford Motor Company . . . a proponent of light, serviceable cars, Ford on Oct. 1, 1908, introduced the Model T and produced in the 19 years that followed over 15 million "Tin Lizzies" . . . 1927 marked the end of "T" production, followed by the Model A . . . Ford established a $5 minimum wage in 1914, increasing it to $6 in 1922, introduced the eight hour day and profit-sharing in 1914, and adopted a 40-hour week in 1926 . . . Mr. Ford played an active role in the management of the Ford Motor Company until 1945, when his grandson, Henry Ford II, was named president of the company.

## GLIDDEN, Charles Jasper

**1857•1927** In 1900 Glidden retired from active business life, having accumulated a comfortable fortune during his association with the Bell Telephone Company . . . in 1903 he made a motor tour of the major countries of Europe, followed a year later by an auto journey around the world, the first of its kind . . . during the latter trip, Glidden conceived the idea of organizing a series of motor tours around the United States to promote the infant auto industry . . . the first Glidden Trophy was awarded to Percy Pierce in 1905, the last to a team of Metz cars in 1913 . . . while in existence the Glidden Tour was conducted annually (with the exception of 1912) and served to capture the imagination of its spectators, while at the same time stimulating their interest in the burgeoning auto industry . . . in his later years he devoted much of his time to promoting interest in aviation.

### GRAHAM, Ray A.

**1887●1932** Along with brothers Robert C. and Joseph C., began in the glass manufacturing business, using machines invented by Joseph . . . while managing the family's farm properties, Ray became interested in the possibilities of light weight trucks and invented a rear axle to be used under a Ford chassis . . . after their glass company merged with the Owens Bottle Company, Joseph and Robert joined Ray to form the Graham Brothers Truck Company, builders of truck bodies . . . in 1921 the brothers made an agreement with Dodge allowing them to build a truck carrying the Graham nameplate, but using Dodge engines and transmissions . . . to keep the arrangement permanent, Dodge bought majority interest in Graham Brothers six months after the original agreement, and the Grahams became officials of Dodge Brothers . . . their association with Dodge was brief, lasting only until 1927 when they left to buy and reorganize Paige-Detroit, forming the Graham-Paige Motors Corporation.

### HAYNES, Elwood G.

**1857●1925** Haynes' car, among the first built in the United States, was constructed with the aid of the Apperson Brothers and successfully tested in 1894 . . . four years later he started Haynes Automobile Company; initially successful, it went out of business in 1925 . . . aside from his manufacturing endeavors, Haynes was a prominent metallurgist, pioneering in the use of aluminum in motor cars as well as in developing several important structural alloys.

## JEFFERY, Thomas B.

**1845●1910** Came to the United States in 1863, and in 1879 began to manufacture bicycles under the trademark "Rambler" . . . Jeffery, who invented the clincher tire in 1881, began experimenting with motor vehicles as early as 1897, but it wasn't until 1900 that he successfully produced one . . . in that year, he sold his bicycle business, and purchased a factory in which he began to manufacture G & J cars (later known as Rambler) cars in 1902 . . . Jeffery remained president of Thomas B. Jeffery Company, later the Nash Motors Company, until his death.

## JORDAN, Edward "Ned"

**1882●1958** Entered the auto industry as advertising manager for the Thomas B. Jeffery Company . . . Jordan remained with the Jeffery Company until 1916, when he organized his own company—the Jordan Motor Car Company . . . although production was low—Jordan refused to build more than 5,000 "Playboys" in any single year—the company always showed a profit, largely as a result of its advertising program . . . instituted by Jordan himself it was the first to stress the esthetic value of the car and make an appeal to the prospective buyer's sense of adventure and glamor . . . the company prospered until the 1929 market crash . . . after the depression, Jordan worked as an advertising consultant, and in 1950 began writing a weekly column in the Automotive News.

## JOY, Henry Bourne

**1864●1936** Served as president of the Fort Street Depot Company from 1896 to 1907 . . . while with Fort Street Depot, Joy became interested in W. D. Packard's auto company, initially as an investor, eventually becoming president of Packard in 1901 . . . while with Packard, he also championed the movement for good roads as president of the Lincoln Highway Association . . . Joy remained president of Packard until 1916, at which time he became chairman of the board . . . ill health forced him to retire several years before his death.

## KETTERING, Charles F.

**1876●1958** Began his career as an engineer for National Cash Register . . . after working at NCR for five years, left to organize Delco Laboratories for the purpose of developing an ignition system . . . one of his first customers was Henry Leland, president of Cadillac, who, after ordering 8,000 ignition systems, later called upon Kettering to perfect the electric self-starter that appeared on the 1911 Cadillac . . . in 1916 he sold his interest in Delco to the United Motors Corporation . . . in 1920, "Boss Ket" became the head of the General Motors research laboratories, contributing toward the development of such things as quick-drying paint and Ethyl gasoline . . . Kettering went into a purely nominal retirement in 1947, remaining with General Motors as a director and research consultant until his death in Dayton, Ohio.

## KING, Charles Brady

**1868•1957** Like Ford, King first became interested in self-propelled vehicles upon seeing one at the 1893 Columbian Exposition, where he had gone to exhibit some of his own inventions . . . preceding the 1896 debut of his first practical vehicle, King, in 1895, had organized American Motor League, a pioneer association to promote better roads . . . King also designed the 1902 "Silent Northern," a vehicle which featured three-point suspension and an integral engine-transmission assembly . . . he organized the King Motor Car Company in 1910, and in 1916 turned his efforts to the design of aircraft engines.

## KNUDSEN, William S.

**1879•1948** Joined the Ford Motor Company in 1912 as manager of the company's 27 plants . . . during World War I, Knudsen was in charge of manufacturing Eagle boats for the Navy . . . before leaving Ford in 1921 he had installed assembly plants in several foreign countries . . . resigned from Ford to become general manager of Ireland and Matthews Manufacturing Company, but in less than a year he was called to Chevrolet Motor Company . . . two years later he became president and general manager of Chevrolet, as well as vice president of General Motors . . . under Knudsen's guidance, Chevrolet in 1928 switched from a four to a six-cylinder engine, and within a year had produced well over a million of the new models . . . after becoming president of General Motors in 1937, Knudsen in 1940 resigned his office to take a position on the National Defense Advisory Commission . . . during the war he served with several government agencies, usually acting as a co-ordinator and general "trouble shooter" . . . so thorough was his work that in 1944, Knudsen, then a three star general, received the Army's Distinguished Service Medal.

## LELAND, Henry M.

**1843•1932** Spent his younger years working in the factories of several well-known firearms manufacturers learning first-hand the technique of parts interchangeability, a method he employed so successfully in the auto industry . . . after a series of ventures that ran from inventing the mechanical hair clipper to manufacturing engines, Leland in 1902 reorganized the Henry Ford Company, which became the Cadillac Motor Car Company . . . while with Cadillac, Leland was responsible for the company's introduction of such innovations as standardized parts, electric starting, and automatic ignition advance . . . Leland left Cadillac in 1917, and some years later organized the Lincoln Motor Car Company, which was purchased by Ford in 1922.

## MACAULEY, Alvan

**1872•1952** Began his career as a patent attorney, holding various positions with National Cash Register and American Arithmometer, predecessor of Burroughs Corporation . . . Macauley joined Packard as general manager in 1910 . . . three years later he was made vice president, and in 1916 became president of Packard . . . under Macauley's guidance, Packard, as well as becoming a leading auto producer, specialized in the development of engines, contributing such things as the Liberty engine of World War I, the first engine specifically designed for a tank, the first production diesel aircraft engine . . . Macauley, a director of the National Automobile Chamber of Commerce from 1913, became its president in 1928, an office he held until 1946 . . . he was made chairman of the board of Packard in 1939, serving in that capacity until retiring in 1948.

## MARMON, Howard C.

**1876•1943** Worked as an associate with his father in a flour mill machinery business that was eventually absorbed in the auto industry . . . became vice president in charge of engineering at the Marmon Motor Company in 1902 . . . designed the Marmon automobile as well as the 1911 Indianapolis Race winning Marmon "Wasp" . . . invented the duplex down draft manifold and pioneered in the use of weight saving aluminum in V-16 engines . . . served as president of the Society of Automobile Engineers during the years 1913–1914, and in 1931 was awarded a medal for the outstanding automotive design of the year, the Marmon Sixteen . . . developed the Liberty engine during World War I . . . selected as the only American honorary member of the British Society of Automotive Engineers.

## MASON, George Walter

**1891•1954** Entered the auto industry in 1913 with Studebaker . . . a year later, he joined Dodge, leaving in 1915 to become purchasing agent for the American Auto Trimming Company . . . during World War I Mason acted as a co-ordinator for the Army Ordnance Department . . . in 1919 accepted a position with Irving National Bank in New York . . . in 1921 Mason returned to the auto industry, taking a position with Maxwell-Chalmers Corporation, then being reorganized by Walter P. Chrysler . . . a year later he was named general works manager, holding that position until leaving Chrysler to become vice president of Copeland Products, Incorporated, in 1926 . . . although elected president of Copeland in 1927, Mason in 1928 left to become president of Kelvinator Corporation . . . in 1936, an offer of the presidency of Nash Motors ultimately resulted in the formation of the Nash-Kelvinator Corporation with Mason as president and Charles

W. Nash board chairman . . . with Nash's death in 1948, Mason, at that time president of the Automobile Manufacturers Association, also became board chairman of N-K . . . when the Nash-Kelvinator-Hudson Motor Car Company merger in 1954 was completed, Mason became president and chairman of the newly formed American Motors Corporation.

### MATHESON, Charles Walter

**1876•1940** With brother Frank built the Matheson Six between 1903 and 1913 . . . in 1921, after spending a year as New York sales representative for Dodge Brothers, Matheson became vice president of that company . . . three years later he became vice president and sales director for General Motors' Oakland Motor Car Company . . . after resigning his post with General Motors, Matheson assumed a similar position with Kelvinator . . . in 1928 he moved on to Chrysler Corporation, becoming vice president in charge of sales . . . ten years later Matheson left Chrysler to become president and general manager of Reo Motor Car Company, a position he held until his death.

### MAXWELL, Jonathan Dixon

**1864•1928** Like many other automobile manufacturers, Maxwell got his start in the bicycle business, operating a repair shop with Elmer Apperson . . . he assisted Elmer Apperson and Elwood Haynes in building the latter's first car . . . in 1903 Maxwell teamed with Benjamin Briscoe to organize the Maxwell-Briscoe Company, producers of a $500 two-cylinder runabout . . . aside from his manufacturing accomplishments, Maxwell was an inventor of note, assisting in the design of the Oldsmobile and Northern automobiles and inventing the thermo-siphon cooling system . . . he served as vice president of the United States Motor Company before retiring from the auto industry in 1913.

## METZ, Charles

**1864•1937** Organized the Waltham Manufacturing Company to build bicycles . . . later associated with the Orient Oil Bicycle and the Orient Buckboard companies . . . in 1909 Metz purchased the Waltham factory, and began to manufacture the low priced Metz "22" . . . a team of three of his cars won the 1913 Glidden Tour with a perfect score . . . throughout his association with the auto industry, Metz championed the movement toward smaller, lower-priced cars, at one time going so far as to devise a plan for shipping component parts to dealers for assembly . . . Metz Company was dissolved in 1922, at which time Mr. Metz retired from the industry.

## NASH, Charles W.

**1864•1948** Started his career working in the Durant-Dort carriage works, where he developed the straight-line conveyor-belt system, a standard item in today's auto assembly plants . . . when Durant left the wagon business to start Buick, Nash went along with him and in 1910 became president of that company . . . Buick so prospered under Nash's leadership that in 1912 he was made president of General Motors, a position he held until 1916 . . . in that year Nash purchased the Thomas B. Jeffery Company and in 1917 began to manufacture Nash cars . . . Nash remained president of the Nash Motor Company until 1930 when he became chairman of the board . . . shortly thereafter, merger negotiations with the Kelvinator Corporation were completed, and the Nash-Kelvinator Corporation was formed with George Mason as president and Charles W. Nash as chairman of the board.

195

## OLDS, Ransom E.

**1864•1950** After successful experiments with steam vehicles as early as 1886, Olds completed his first gasoline powered vehicle in 1894 . . . encouraged by the interest shown in his vehicle, Olds organized Olds Motor Vehicle Company in 1897 . . . this first endeavor was not successful; the company was reorganized in 1899 as the Olds Motor Works . . . in 1901 Olds developed his famous "curved dash runabout" priced at $650, making it the first really low-priced car . . . after a 1901 fire destroyed the Detroit plant, the company moved to its Lansing location . . . two years later Olds sold his interest in the Olds Motor Works, later Olds Division of General Motors, and organized the Reo Motor Car Company . . . seemingly not content with founding an industry, Olds continued his experiments with the internal combustion engine, contributing, among other things, the first practical power mower.

## PACKARD, James Ward

**1863•1928** Organized the Packard Electric Company in 1890 . . . by 1893 Packard had drawn the plans for his first auto, but financial difficulties delayed its production until 1899 . . . after experiments with the initial car proved successful, Packard in 1900 organized New York and Ohio Automobile Co. . . . with increased capital, the company moved to Detroit in 1903 and became Packard Motor Company . . . Mr. Packard, prior to this time president, became chairman of the board, a post which he held until retiring in 1915.

## PAIGE, Fred O.

**1864•1935** Organized Paige-Detroit Motor Company in 1909 to produce two-cycle automobiles . . . Paige was president of the company until 1910, at which time Harry Jewett assumed control . . . in 1927 the Graham Brothers acquired control of Jewett's interests, and the company became Graham-Paige.

## POPE, Albert Augustus

**1843•1909** After serving in the Civil War, Pope organized in 1879 a company to manufacture bicycles, a venture which was to earn for him the title "the founder of American bicycle industries" . . . following his highly successful bicycle ventures, Pope began to manufacture electric runabouts through the Columbia Electric Company in 1896 . . . within a few years, he controlled the Pope-Toledo, Pope-Harford, and Pope-Waverly Companies . . . however, with auto success on one hand, Pope faced a crisis on the other in the form of a decline of his bicycle business, eventually forcing the Pope Manufacturing Company into receivership.

## SELDEN, George Baldwin

**1846•1932** A veteran of the Civil War, he became a patent attorney in 1871 . . . having a keen interest in mechanics, Selden unsuccessfully experimented with engines of his own design during the years 1873–1875 . . . by 1876, he was working on the design for a self-propelled vehicle using an engine operating on the Brayton cycle . . . Selden had developed a three-cylinder-Brayton type engine by 1877, and proceeded to design the road locomotive disclosed in his patent application of May 8, 1879 . . . although never successful in obtaining the funds to build the proposed machine, Selden was granted his patent—No. 549,160 "Road Machine" Nov. 5, 1895 . . . on Nov. 4, 1899, he sold the patent on a royalty basis to W. C. Whitney of Columbia Electric who successfully brought suit against a number of

197

automobile manufacturers before the now historic appeal judgment Jan. 11, 1911 (Electric Vehicle Company vs. C. A. Buerr) wherein the patent was held valid but not infringed by virtue of the fact that all manufacturers were using Otto, not Brayton, type engines . . . Selden unsuccessfully entered other auto firms before his death.

### STANLEY, Brothers Francis E. and Freelan O.

Francis **1849•1918**, Freelan **1849•1940** In 1893, the twin brothers invented the Stanley dry plate process which revolutionized photography . . . they were co-designers of the Stanley Steamer—1897—and the world-record-holding steamer of 1906 (Ormond Beach, 127.66 m.p.h.) . . . as owners of the Stanley Motor Company they directed the business until retiring in 1917.

### STUDEBAKER, John Mohler

**1833•1917** In 1858 bought brother Henry's share of the Studebaker Brothers (Wagon) Company which then became C. (for brother Clem) and J. M. Studebaker Company . . . the company entered the auto industry as a body maker in 1899 . . . in 1902 produced its first vehicle, an electric car . . . in 1908 Studebaker contracted to market the entire output of the E-M-F Company . . . in 1911 the two firms merged to form the Studebaker Corporation, which produced the first car with a Studebaker name plate in 1912 . . . John M. Studebaker served as chairman of the corporation until his death.

### STUTZ, Harry C.

**1871•1930** After winning recognition among the early auto manufacturers with the invention of an improved rear axle, Stutz became successively sales manager for the Schebler

Carburetor Company, engineer for the Marion Motor Car Company, and designer of the famous "American Underslung" for the American Motor Car Company . . . in 1910 he entered into the Stutz Motor Parts Company and in 1911 organized the Ideal Motor Company to manufacture Stutz cars . . . two years later the companies merged to form the Stutz Motor Car Company with Stutz as president . . . although he sold his interest in Stutz Motor Car Company in 1919, Harry Stutz later joined Henry Campbell, his partner in the Stutz Motor Parts Company, in the H.C.S. Motor Car Company, again as president . . . Stutz remained president of H.C.S. until his retirement.

## THOMAS, Edwin Ross

**1850●1936** Started the E. R. Thomas Motor Company of Buffalo in 1900 . . . the company was quite successful, and Thomas remained its president until his decision to retire in 1911, when he sold his holding to the United States Motor Company . . . although successful as an auto maker, Thomas probably gained his greatest fame as the designer-builder of the "Thomas Flyer," winner of the 1908 New York to Paris (via California, Siberia and Europe) Race . . . despite the fact that he officially retired in 1911, Thomas was active in numerous enterprises until his death.

## WHITE BROTHERS, Windsor T., Rollin H., Walter C.

Windsor **1866●1958**, Rollin **1872●1962**, Walter **1876●1929** The brothers began their careers working for the White Sewing Machine Company, owned by their father . . . Rollin and Windsor did experimental work on steam engines and produced the first steam powered White automobile in 1900 . . . in 1901 Walter was sent to London to demonstrate the car and establish a niche in the European market . . . he returned to the United States in 1904 and continued to demonstrate the company's vehicles in races and hill climbs . . . in 1906 the White Company was organized, with Windsor as president, to handle the automotive line . . . the brothers introduced their first gasoline car in 1909, and in 1910, their first gasoline powered truck . . . in 1915 the White Motor Company was formed with Windsor as president . . . Rollin left the company in 1914, founded the Cleveland Plow Company and manufactured tractors . . . he re-entered the automotive industry in 1923 producing the Rollin car until 1925 . . . in 1921 Walter assumed the presidency of the White Motor Company as Windsor was made Chairman of the Board.

## WILLS, Childe Harold

**1878●1940** Spent the years 1900–1903 working for the Boyer Machine Company and nights as a draftsman for Henry Ford's new organization . . . when the Ford Motor Company was formed, Wills was made production manager and chief engineer . . . he gained fame from his development of the use of vanadium steel for commercial purposes, and is credited with introducing molybdenum steel in auto construction . . . in 1919 Wills, by then a millionaire, left Ford, and in 1920 organized his own company, Wills-St. Claire . . . never particularly successful, the company went out of business in 1927 . . . in 1933, Wills became chief metallurgist for Chrysler, a position he held until his death.

## WILLYS, John North

**1873●1933** In 1906 he organized the American Motor Car Sales Company to sell the entire output of the Overland Company . . . during panic of 1907 he acquired the manufacturing facilities of the Pope-Toledo Company in an effort to revive the sinking Overland concern . . . the company was moved to Toledo with Willys as president and in 1908 the production of Willys-Overland totaled 4,000 units . . . by 1915 Willys-Overland production reached 94,500, second only to Ford . . . after a post-war bankruptcy threat was averted by Walter P. Chrysler, the company prospered, and in 1929 John N. Willys sold his holdings for $21 million . . . hard times after the market crash prompted Willys to return to the company in 1932, but his attempts to save it from bankruptcy were unsuccessful, and Willys-Overland went into receivership in 1933 . . . in 1953 the firm became part of Kaiser Industries Corporation.

## WINTON, Alexander

**1860•1932** Started the Winton Bicycle Company in 1890, ten years after his arrival in the United States . . . in 1896 Winton built his first car, which he sold to a Pennsylvania engineer the following year . . . he organized the Winton Motor Carriage Company in 1897 . . . by 1905 he had produced an eight-cylinder motor vehicle, presumably one of the first . . . other contributions to the industry include the development of a practical storage battery, design of a successful speed governor, and four years before his death, perfection of a light, oil burning aircraft engine . . . he remained president of the Winton Motor Car Company until it suspended production in 1924 . . . organized the Winton Engine Company which made marine, rail and industrial diesel engines— the latter firm was purchased by General Motors in 1930 and became the Cleveland Diesel Division.

# roll call

More than 3,000 makes of cars and trucks have been produced by some 1,500 manufacturers in the United States since the dawn of the auto age. Some were trial models, some were produced for one year only, others have a longer story. Listed below are the names of the more than 3,000 makes that can be documented. The beginning year and, where available, the last year of production also are shown.

## A

A.B.C.—1906–1911
A.B.C.—1922
A.B.C.—1939
A.B.C. Steamer—1901
Abbott—1909–1918
Abbott Cleveland—1917
Abbott-Detroit—1909
Abbott-Downing—1919
Abenaque—1900
Abendroth & Root—1907–1913
Able—1916
Abresch-Cramer—1910–1911
Acadia—1904
Acason—1915–1926
Ace—1919–1922
Ace Truck—1919–1923
A.C.F.—1926
Acme—1902–1903

Acme—1903–1910
Acorn—1910
Acorn Truck—1925
Adams—1906–1907
Adams—1911–1912
Adams—1924
Adams-Farwell—1903–1913
Adelphia—1921
Adette—1947
Admiral—1914
Adria—1921
Adrian—1902–1903
Advance—1910
A.E.C.—1914–1916
Aero—1921
Aerocar—1905–1908
Aerocar—1948
Aerocar—1950

Aero Type—1921
Aetna—1915
Aetna—1922
Ahrens-Fox—1911-1933
A.I.C.—1913*
Airphibian—1946; 1952
Airscoot—1947*
Airway—1948-1949
Ajax—1901-1903
Ajax—1914*
Ajax—1920-1921
Ajax—1925-1926
Ajax Electric—1901-1903
Akron—1901*
Akron—1913*
Akron—1912-1913
Alamobile—1902*
Aland—1917*
Albany—1907-1908
Alco—1905-1914
Alco Truck—1910-1914
Aldo—1910*
Aldrich—1897-1898
Alena—1922
Algonquin—1913
All American—1919
All American—1923
Allegheny—1908
Allen—1914-1922
Allen & Clark—1908-1909
Allen Cyclecar—1914*
Allen-Kingston—1907-1910
Allfour—1919*
Allis-Chalmers—1914-1917
Allith—1908
All Power—1917-1921
All State—1951-1953

Alma—1913
Alpena—1911-1913
Alpena—1912
Alsace—1919-1920
Alstel—1915-1917
Alter—1915-1917
Altha Electric—1900-1901
Altham—1896-1901
Altman—1898
Alxo—1905*
Amalgamated—1905*
Ambassador—1921-1925
Amco—1917-1921
America—1911*
American—1900-1903
American Austin—1930-1937
American Auto—1904*
American Auto Vehicle—1907*
American Bantam—1937-1941
American Beauty—1915-1916
American Beauty—1920-1921
American Berliet—1905-1907
American Chocolate—1903-1906
American Coulthard—1905-1907
American Electric—1899-1900
American Fiat—1915
American Gas—1895
American Knight—1919*
American LaFrance Truck—1910
American Mercedes—1905-1907
American Mors—1906-1909
American Motor—1902-1903
American Motor—1905-1906
American Motor Truck—1906-1911
American Napier—1904
American Populaire—1904*
American Power Carriage—1900*

*Only year produced

American Simplex—1905–1910
American Six—1916–1917
American Southern—1921*
American Steam—1922–1923
American Steamer—1900
American Tri-Car—1912*
American Underslung—1906–1914
American Voiturette—1899*
Americar (Willys)—1940–1942
Ames—1898
Ames—1910–1916
Amesbury—1898*
Amos—1913*
Amoskeag Fire Engine—1867–1906
Amplex—1910–1915
Ams-Sterling—1917*
Anchor—1909–1911
Anderson—1908*
Anderson—1916–1925
Anderson Electric—1907–1919
Andover—1914–1917
Andrews—1895*
Anhut—1910–1911
Ann Arbor—1911
Annhauser-Busch Truck—1905
Ansted—1927
Anthony—1897
Apex—1920–1922
Apollo—1906–1907
Appel—1909
Apperson—1902–1925
Apple—1909
Apple—1915–1916
Appleton—1922
Arbenz—1911–1918
Arcadia—1911*
Ardsley—1905–1906

Argo-Borland Electric—1914
Argo-Case—1905*
Argo Electric—1911–1916
Argo Gas—1914
Argonne Four—1919–1921
Ariel—1905–1907
Ariston—1906*
Aristos—1913
Armleder—1914
Arnold Electric—1895
Arrow—1914
Artzberger—1904
Aster—1906–1907
Astor—1925
Astra—1920
Atco—1920–1922
Atlantic—1915
Atlas—1904–1913
Atlas—1907
Atlas-Knight—1911
Atlas Truck—1918
Atterbury Truck—1915
Auburn—1903–1936
Auglaize Truck—1912
Aultman—1901
Aurora—1906–1908
Austin—1903–1920
Austin—1930
Austin Steamer—1894
Auto-Acetylene—1899
Auto-Bug—1910
Autobuggy—1906
Autocar—1897–1912
Autocar Truck—1908
Autocycle—1907
Auto Dynamic—1901
Auto Fore Car—1900

*Only year produced

Auto-Go—1900
Autohorse—1917–1921
Auto-King—1900*
Automatic—1906
Automatic—1921–1925
Automobile Forecarriage—1900
Automobile Voiturette—1900
Automotor—1901–1904
Auto Motor—1912
Auto Red Bug—1924
Auto-Tricar—1914
Autotwo—1900
Auto Vehicle—1903
Available Truck—1910
Avanti (Studebaker)—1962–1966†
Avanti II (Avanti Motor Corporation)—1965 to date
Average Man's Runabout—1906
Avery—1921
Avery Tractor—1942
Avery Truck—1912–1916

# B

Babcock—1910–1912
Babcock—1914
Babcock Electric—1906–1912
Bachelles Electric—1901
Backhus—1925
Bacon—1905
Badger—1910–1912
Bailey—1907–1910
Bailey-Electric—1907–1915
Bailey-Klapp—1915
Bailey-Perking—1907
Baker-Bell—1913–1914
Baker Electric—1899–1915

Baker & Elberg Electric—1894
Baker R & L Electric—1915–1920
Baker-Steam—1917
Baker Steamer—1921–1923
Balboa—1924
Baldner—1902–1906
Baldwin—1900–1901
Ball—1902
Ballard—1894
Baltimore—1900*
Balzer—1894
Banker—1905*
Banker Bros.—1896
Banker Electric—1905
Banner—1915*
Bantam—1914*
Barbarino—1923
Barby—1910
Barker—1912
Barley—1922
Barley—1905–1924
Barlow—1922
Barnes—1905*
Barnes—1912
Barnhart—1905
Barracuda (Plymouth)—1964 to date
Barrett & Perret Electric—1895
Barrows Electric—1897
Barrows Motor Vehicle—1897
Bartholomew—1901–1920
Bartlett—1921
Barver—1925
Bateman—1917
Bates—1903–1905
Bauer—1914

*Only year produced
†U.S. production terminated December 1963

Bauer—1925
Bauroth—1899
Bay State—1906–1907
Bay State—1922–1923
Bayard—1903
B.D.A.C.—1904
Beacon—1933
Beacon Flyer—1908
Beardsley—1901–1902
Beardsley Electric—1914–1917
Beau-Chamberlain—1901
Beaver—1913–1923
Beck—1921
Bedelia—1909
Beebe—1907
Beech Creek—1915–1919
Beggs—1918–1923
B.E.L.—1921–1923
Belden—1907–1910
Bellefontaine—1908–1917
Bell—1907*
Bell—1913
Bell—1911–1923
Belmont—1908
Belmont—1910
Belmont—1912
Belmont—1916
Bemmel & Burnham—1908*
Bendix—1907–1909
Benham—1914*
Ben-Hur—1917
Benner—1908–1909
Benson—1901
Benton—1913*
Benton Harbor Motor Carriage—
    1896
Berg—1902–1907

Bergdoll—1910–1913
Berkley—1907
Berkshire—1905–1912
Berliet—1905
Bertolet—1908–1912
Berwick Electric—1926
Bessemer Truck—1922
Best—1900
Bethlehem—1906–1908
Bethlehem—1917
Betz—1919
Beverly—1905–1907
Bewis—1915
Bewman—1912
Beyster-Detroit—1910–1911
B.F.—1912
Bi-Autogo (Scripps Booth)—1913
Bi-Car—1912
Biddle—1915–1920
Biddle—1920
Biddle-Crane—1922–1923
Biddle-Murray—1906–1908
Biederman Truck—1921
Billy—1910
Bimel—1911
Bimel—1915–1917
Binney-Burnham—1902
Birch—1917–1922
Bird—1896–1897
Birmingham—1921–1922
Birnel—1911
Black—1891
Black—1907–1910
Black Crow—1907
Black Crow—1909
Black Diamond—1904–1905
Blackhawk—1903

*Only year produced

Blackhawk—1929–1931
Blackstone—1916*
Blair—1911
Blaisdell—1903
Blakeslee Electric—1906
Blemline—1898
Bliss—1906*
B.L.M.—1906–1907
B.L.M.C.—1907–1909
Block Bros.—1905
Blomstrom—1904–1906
Blood—1905*
Blue Streak—1908
Bluffelimber—1901
Blumberg—1918
Board—1912
Bobbi-Car—1947
Boggs—1903*
Boisselot—1901
Bollee—1908*
Bollstrom—1920
Bolte—1901*
Booth—1896
Borbein—1904–1908
Borland Electric—1913
Borland-Grannis—1912–1916
Boss—1903–1909
Boston—1900*
Boston Electric—1907
Boston & Amesbury—1902
Boston-Haynes Apperson—1898
Boston High Wheel—1908*
Bour-Davis—1915–1923
Bourne—1917
Bouronville—1921–1922
Bowling Green—1912
Bowman—1921

Boyd—1911
Boynton—1922*
Bradfield—1929
Bradford—1920
Bradley—1920
Bramwell—1902–1903
Bramwell-Robinson—1899
Brasie Cyclecar—1914*
Brasie Truck—1915–1916
Brazier—1902–1904
Brecht—1901–1902
Breer Steam Car—1900
Breeze & Lawrence—1905
Bremac—1923*
Brennan—1908
Brew-Hatcher—1904–1905
Brewster—1934–1936
Brewster-Knight—1916–1925
Bridgeport—1922
Briggs—1933
Briggs-Detroiter—1910–1918
Briggs & Stratton—1922
Brighton—1896
Brighton—1914
Brightwood—1912
Brintel—1912*
Briscoe—1914
Bristol—1902–1903
Bristol—1908
Broc Electric—1909–1916
Brock—1920–1921
Brockville-Atlas—1911
Brockway Truck—1912
Brodesser Truck—1909
Brogan—1946
Brook—1920–1921
Brooks—1908

*Only year produced

Brooks Steamer—1924
Brown—1899–1900
Brown—1909*
Brown—1912
Brown—1914
Brown—1916
Brown—1922
Brown Steamer—1888
Brown's Touring Cart—1898
Brown-Burtt—1904
Brownell—1910
Brownie—1915
Browniekar—1908
Brunn—1906–1910
Brunner Truck—1910
Brunswick—1916
Brush Runabout—1906–1912
Brush Truck—1907
Bryan Steam—1918
Buck—1925
Buckeye—1905–1917
Buckeye Gas Buggy—1895
Buckles—1914
Buckmobile—1903–1904
Buddie—1921
Buddy—1925
Buffalo—1900–1902
Buffalo—1907*
Buffalo—1912–1915
Buffalo Electric—1900–1912
Buffington—1900*
Buffum—1900–1906
Buffman—1900
Bug—1914
Buggyaut—1909
Buggycar—1907–1910
Bugmobile—1907–1909

Buick—1903 to date
Bull Dog—1924
Bundy Steam Wagon—1895
Burdick—1909–1911
Burford—1916
Burg—1910–1915
Burns—1909–1912
Burroughs—1914
Burrows—1915*
Burtt—1917–1923
Bus—1917
Bush—1917–1923
Bushbury—1897
Bushnell—1912
Busser—1915
Butler—1914
Buzmobile—1917*
Byrider—1908–1909
Byron—1912
B.Z.T.—1915

## C

Cadillac—1902 to date
California—1912
California Cyclecar—1914*
Californian 1922
Call—1911
Calorie—1904
Calvert—1927
Camaro (Chevrolet)—1966 to date
Cameron—1907–1920
Cameron—1914
Cameron—1920
Campbell—1917–1919
Canada—1911
Canadian—1921
Canda—1900–1901

*Only year produced

209

Cannon—1904
Cantone—1905
Cantono Electric—1905–1907
Capital—1902
Capitol—1912
Capitol—1920
Carbon—1902
Car DeLuxe—1907
Cardway—1923
Carhart Steamer—1872
Carhartt—1911–1916
Carlson—1904–1910
Carnation—1913–1915
Carnegie—1915–1916
Carpenter Electric—1895
Carrison—1908
Carroll—1912–1913
Carroll Six—1920–1921
Carter—1907–1912
Carter—1916*
Cartercar—1908–1915
Cartermobile—1924
Carthage—1924*
Casco—1926
Case—1910
Case—1920
Casey—1914
Cass—1915
Cato—1907
Cavac—1910
Cavalier—1913
Cavalier—1927
Caward-Dart—1924
Cawley—1917*
C.B.—1917
Ceco—1914
Celt—1927*

Centaur—1902–1903
Central—1905
Central Steam—1905–1906
Century—1900–1904
Century—1927
Century Electric—1901
Century Electric—1912–1916
Century Steam—1901
C.F.—1908
C.G.V.—1903
 (Charron, Girardot and Voight)
Chadwick—1906–1916
Chalfant—1906–1912
Chalmers—1910–1923
Chalmers-Detroit—1908–1910
Champion—1902
Champion—1909
Champion—1915*
Champion—1921–1925
Champion Electric—1899
Chandler—1913–1928
Chapman—1899–1901
Charger (Dodge)—1965 to date
Charter Car—1904
Charter Oak—1917
Chase—1907
Chatham—1907
Checker Cab—1921 to date
Chelsea—1901–1904
Chelsea—1915*
Chevelle (Chevrolet)—1963 to date
Chevrolet—1909
Chevrolet—1911 to date
Chevrolet Truck—1918 to date
Chevy II (Chevrolet)—1961 to date
Chicago—1899–1905
Chicago—1906*

*Only year produced

Chicago—1907–1910
Chicago—1917
Chicago Commercial—1905–1907
Chicago Electric—1912–1914
Chicago Motor Buggy—1908*
Chicago Steamer—1905
Chief—1908–1909
Chief—1947
Christie—1904–1909
Christman—1901–1902
Christopher—1908–1910
Chrysler—1924 to date
Church—1901*
Church—1902*
Church—1902–1903
Church—1910–1911
Church—1914*
Church Electric—1912–1913
Churchfield—1911–1915
Cincinnati—1903
Cino—1909–1913
Circa-Hermann—1914
Cla-Holme—1923*
Clapps Motor Carriage—1898
Clark—1898–1903
Clark—1903*
Clarke Carter—1909–1913
Clark Electric—1912
Clark-Hatfield—1908–1909
Clarkmobile—1903–1907
Clarkspeed—1926
Clark Steamer—1901
Classic—1917–1920
Classic—1921
Clear & Dunham—1905
Cleburne—1912
Clegg Steamer—1885*

Clendon—1908
Clermont—1903
Clermont Steamer—1922
Cletrac Truck—1922*
Cleveland—1902–1903
Cleveland—1908–1909
Cleveland—1904–1909
Cleveland—1919–1925
Cleveland Cycle Car—1913
Cleveland Electric—1900
Climax—1907
Climber—1919–1923
Clinton—1923
Cloughley—1902–1903
Club Car—1911
Clyde—1919
Clydesdale Truck—1914
Clymer—1908
Coates-Goshen—1908–1911
Coats Steam—1922–1923
Cobra (Shelby American)—1962 to
    date
Coey—1911
Coey Flyer—1913*
Cogswell—1912
Colburn—1907–1911
Colby—1911–1913
Colby—1914
Cole—1909–1925
Coleman Truck—1928
Collier—1917
Collinet—1922
Collins—1920–1921
Collins Electric—1901
Colly—1901*
Colonial—1921–1922
Colonial Electric—1912–1913

*Only year produced

211

Colonial Electric—1917–1918
Colt—1908*
Colt Truck—1908*
Columbia—1899*
Columbia—1900–1907
Columbia—1916–1924
Columbia-Dauman—1900
Columbia Electric—1895
Columbia Electric—1899–1904
Columbia Electric—1906–1918
Columbia Gas—1900
Columbia-Knight—1911
Columbia Motor Carriage—1897
Columbia & Riker—1901
Columbia Steamer—1900
Columbia Taxicab—1915
Columbia Truck—1916–1920
Columbia Wagonette—1901
Columbus—1902–1904
Columbus Electric—1906
Comet—1907
Comet—1916–1936
Comet—1917–1922
Comet (3-wh.)—1946
Comet Cyclecar—1914
Comet Electric—1921
Comet (Ford)—1960 to date
Commander—1921
Commander—1922
Commer—1912
Commerce—1916
Commercial—1902–1909
Commercial—1903–1905
Commercial—1904
Commercial—1906–1907
Commercial—1927
Commodore—1921–1922

Commonwealth—1903
Commonwealth—1917–1921
Compound—1904
Concord—1916
Condor Truck—1929
Conestoga—1918
Conklin Electric—1895
Connecticut—1908*
Connersville—1914
Conover—1907–1908
Conrad—1900–1903
Consolidated—1904–1905
Consolidated—1916
Consolidated—1903–1906
Continental—1907–1908
Continental—1908*
Continental—1909
Continental—1912
Continental—1914–1915
Continental—1915*
Continental—1933–1934
Continental Mark II (Ford)—1955–1957
Cook—1908–1909
Cook—1921
Copley Minor—1907*
Coppock—1907–1912
Corbett—1907
Corbin—1903–1912
Corbitt—1911–1914
Cord—1929–1932; 1935–1937
Corinthian—1922–1923
Corl—1911*
Corliss—1917
Cornelian—1913
Cornish-Friedberg—1908
Correia—1908–1914

*Only year produced

212

Correja—1911

Cort—1914

Cortland—1911

Cortland—1916–1924

Cortez—1947

Corvair (Chevrolet)—1959 to date

Corvette (Chevrolet)—1953 to date

Corweg—1947*

Corwin—1905–1907

Cosmopolitan—1897–1910

Co-Tay—1920

Cotta—1901

Cougar (Mercury)—1966 to date

Country Club—1904*

Couple-Gear—1905

Courier—1904

Courier—1909–1912

Courier—1922–1926

Covel Electric—1912

Covert Motorette—1902–1907

Covic—1930

Coyote—1909

C.P.—1908

C.P. Truck—1909–1914

Craig-Hunt—1920

Craig-Toledo—1906–1907

Crane—1912–1915

Crane & Breed—1912

Crane-Simplex—1915–1917

Crane-Simplex—1923–1924

Crawford—1905–1930

Crescent—1905

Crescent—1907–1908

Crescent—1914

Crescent—1915*

Crescent—1900–1918

Crescent—1923

Cresson—1915

Crestmobile—1901–1905

Cricket—1914

Criterion—1912

Croce—1914

Crock—1909

Croesus Jr.—1906

Crofton "Bug"—1959

Crompton—1903

Crosley—1939–1952

Cross Steam Carriage—1897

Crouch—1900*

Crow—1910–1922

Crow-Elkhart—1911

Crowdus—1901

Crown—1908–1910

Crown-Magnetic—1920

Crowther-Duryea—1915–1918

Croxton—1911

Croxton-Keeton—1909–1914

Crusader—1923

Crusier—1918–1919

Cucmobile—1907

Cull—1901

Culver—1905

Cummins—1930

Cunningham—1909–1933

Cunningham—1951

Cunningham Steamer—1901

Curran—1928

Curtis—1921–1922

Curtis Steamer—1866

Curtis Truck—1915–1916

Custer—1921

Cutting—1909–1913

C.V.I.—1907–1908

Cyclecar—1914

*Only year produced

Cyclomobile—1920
Cycleplane—1914–1915
Cyclone—1921

# D

D.A.C.—1923
Dagmar—1923–1930
Dain—1912
Daimler (U.S.)—1900–1907
Daley Steam Wagon—1893
Dalton—1911
Daniels—1912
Daniels—1915–1923
Danielson—1914
Dan Patch—1911
Darby—1909–1910
Darling—1901
Darling—1917*
Darrin—1946
Darrow—1903*
Dart—1911
Dart (Chrysler)—1959 to date
Dart Truck—1916
Dartmobile—1922
Davenport—1902
Davids—1902*
DaVinci—1925*
Davis—1909
Davis—1911–1928
Davis—1947–1950
Davis Cycle Car—1913
Dawson—1904*
Day—1911–1914
Day Elder Truck—1919
Dayton—1904–1912
Dayton—1909*
Dayton—1911–1914

Day Utility—1914–1916
Deal—1908–1911
Dearborn—1910–1911
Dearborn—1919
Decatur—1912
Decauville—1909–1912
Decker—1902–1903
Decross—1914
De Dion Bouton—1888–1904
DeDion Motorette—1900
Deemotor—1923
Deemster—1923
Deere—1916
Deere-Clark—1906–1907
Deering—1918
Deering Magnetic—1918
Defiance—1919
DeKalb—1915
Delage—1922
De LaVergne Motor Drag—1896
DeLuxe—1907
Delia Truck—1916*
Delling Steam Car—1924–1929
Del Mar—1949
Delmore—1923
Delta—1916*
Deltal—1914
DeLuxe—1906–1909
DeMartini—1919
DeMats—1905
DeMot—1910–1911
DeMotte—1904*
Denby—1922
Deneen—1917
Denegre—1920
Dependable—1919
Derain—1911*

*Only year produced

Derby—1924
Desberon—1901
Desert Flyer—1908
DeSchaum—1908–1910
DeShaw—1910*
De Sota (Zimmerman)—1913
De Soto—1913
De Soto (Chrysler)—1928–1960
De Tamble—1909
De Tamble—1912
Detroit—1904–1907
Detroit—1905–1907
Detroit—1916
Detroit Air Cooled—1923
Detroit-Chatham—1912
Detroit-Dearborn—1909
Detroit Electric—1906–1923
Detroit Electric—1930
Detroit Oxford—1906–1907
Detroit Speedster—1914
Detroit Steamer—1918
Detroit Steamer—1922
Detroiter—1912
DeVaux—1931–1932
Dewabout—1899
Dey—1895
Dial—1923
Diamond—1907
Diamond-Arrow—1907*
Diamond T. Passenger—1905–1911
Diamond T. Truck—1911 to date
Diana—1925
Dickson Steamer Truck—1865
Dictator—1913
Diebel—1900–1901
Diehl—1923
Differential—1921

Differential—1932
Dile—1914–1916
Dillon Steam—1920*
Direct Drive—1907
Disbrow—1917–1918
Dispatch—1911–1919
Dispatch—1916
Divco Truck—1927
Dixie—1912
Dixie—1917
Dixie Flyer—1916–1924
Dixie Tourist—1908–1910
Dixon—1922
Doane Truck—1929
Doble-Detroit—1919
Doble Steam Car—1918–1929
Dodge—1914 to date
Dodge-Graham—1929
Dodgeson Eight—1926*
Dodo—1909
Dolly Madison—1915
Dolson—1904–1907
Dolson—1906
D'olt—1921–1926
Dorris—1905–1925
Dorris Truck—1919
Dort—1915–1924
Double Drive—1920
Douglass—1918–1919
Dover—1929
Dowagiac—1908
Downing—1914–1917
Downing-Detroit—1913*
Doyle—1900*
Dragon—1906–1908
Dragon—1921*
Drake—1921

*Only year produced

Drednot—1913
Drexel—1916–1917
Driggs—1921–1923
Driggs-Seabury—1915
Drummond—1916*
Duck—1913
Dudgeon Steam—1857
Dudley—1914*
Dudley Electric—1915*
Duer—1907–1910
Duer—1925
Duesenberg—1920–1937
Dumont—1902
Dunmore—1917–1918
Dunn—1914–1917
Duplex—1908–1909
duPont—1919–1932
Duquesne—1903–1906
Duquesne—1905–1906
Duquesne—1912
Durable Dayton—1916
Durant—1921–1931
Duyo—1914
Durocar—1907
Duryea Lightcar—1915*
Duryea—1893–1897
Duryea—1907–1912
Duryea-Gem—1917*
Dusseau—1912
Duty—1920
Dyke—1902–1904
Dymaxion—1933–1935

# E

Eagle—1906*
Eagle—1906–1907
Eagle—1909*

Eagle—1924
Eagle Cyclecar—1914–1915
Eagle-Macomber—1917
Eagle Rotary—1917–1918
Earl—1907–1908
Earl—1921–1923
Eastern—1910*
Eastern Dairies—1925
Eastman—1899
Easton—1907–1913
Eaton—1898
Eck—1903
Eclipse—1901–1902
Eclipse—1908*
Economy—1906
Economy—1908–1911
Economy—1917–1922
Economycar—1914
Eddy—1902
Edmond—1900
Edsel (Ford)—1957–1959
Edwards-Knight—1912–1914
E.H.V.—1903–1906
Eichstaedt—1902
E.I.M.—1916
Eisenhuth—1896
Eisenhuth-Compound—1903
Elbert—1915–1916
Elbert Cyclecar—1914–1915
Elcar—1909–1931
Elcar-Lever—1930
Elco—1915
Elcurto—1921
Eldredge—1903
Eldridge Truck—1913
Electra—1913
Electric Vehicle—1897

*Only year produced

Electric Wagon—1897*
Electrobat—1895
Electrocar—1922
Electronomic—1901
Electruck—1924
Elgin—1916–1924
Elinore—1903
Elite—1906
Elite—1909
Elite Steamer—1901
Elk—1913
Eklhart—1908–1911
Elkhart—1910–1916
Elkhart—1922
Elliot—1897
Elliot—1902
Ellis—1901
Ellsworth—1908
Ellsworth—1917
Elmira—1920
Elmore—1901–1912
Elston—1895
Elvick—1895
Elwell-Parker—1909
Elysee—1926
Emancipator—1909*
Emblem—1910
Embree-McLean—1910*
Emerson—1907
Emmerson & Fisher Motor Wagon
—1896
E.M.F.—1908–1912
Empire—1898*
Empire—1914
Empire—1910–1919
Empire State—1901*
Empress—1906

E.M.S.—1908
Endurance-Steam—1922–1923
Enger—1909
Enger-Everitt—1906–1917
Englehardt—1901
Engler—1914
Enkel Truck—1915*
Entz—1914
Epperson—1912
Erbes—1915–1916
Erie—1897
Erie—1916–1919
Erie—1920
Erie & Sturgis—1897
Ernst—1896
Erskine—1926–1930
Erving—1911–1913
Ess. Eff.—1912*
Essex—1906–1908
Essex Steam Car—1901
Essex (Hudson)—1919–1932
Etnyre—1910–1911
Euclid—1907*
Eugol—1921
Eureka—1907–1909
Eureka—1909
Eureka—1907*
Evans—1904
Evans—1912
Evans—1914
Evansville—1907–1911
Evansville—1914–1917
Everitt—1909
Everitt—1911
Everybody's—1908–1909
Ewing—1908–1910
Excelsior—1910

*Only year produced

# F

F-85 (Oldsmobile)—1960 to date
Facto—1920
Fageol—1916
Fageolbus—1916
Fairbanks-Morse—1909
Fairmount—1906–1907
Falcon—1908
Falcar—1909
F.A.L.—1909–1914
Falcon—1914
Falcar—1922
Falcon—1922
Falcon—1938–1943
Falcon Cycle Car—1913–1914
Falcon (Ford)—1959 to date
Falcon-Knight—1926–1929
Famous—1908–1909
Famous—1917
Fanning Electric—1902–1903
Fargo—1913
Fargo Truck—1929 to date
Farmack—1915–1916
Farmer—1907
Farmobile—1908
Farner—1922
Fauber Auto Cycle Car—1914
Fay (Gr. Pa.)—1912
Federal—1907–1909
Federal—1909
Federal Steamer—1905
Federal Truck—1910
Fee—1908–1909
Fenton—1914
Fergus—1917
Fergus—1920–1921
Ferris—1920–1922

Fiat—1915
Fidelity—1909*
Field Steam—1887
Fifth Avenue Coach—1924
Finch—1902
Findley—1910
Findley—1912
Firestone-Columbus—1907
Fischer—1902–1904
Fischer—1914
Fish—1908
Fisher—1924
Fisher Steamer Truck—1865
Flagler—1914
Flanders—1910
Flanders Electric—1911
Flanders Electric—1915–1916
Fleetruck—1926–1927
Flexbi—1904
Flexible—1932
Flint—1902–1904
Flint—1910–1912
Flint—1923
Flyer—1913
Flyer—1933
Flying Auto—1947
Flying Auto—1950
Fool-Proof—1912
Foos—1913
Ford—1896*
Ford—1903 to date
Fordmobile—1903
Forest—1902
Forest City—1906–1909
Forster Six—1920
Fort Pitt—1908–1911
Fort Wayne—1911

*Only year produced

Foster Steam—1900–1903
Fostoria—1906–1907
Fostoria—1916
Fournier—1902
Four Traction—1907–1909
Four Wheel Drive—1902–1907
Four-Wheel Drive Truck—1912 to date
Fox—1921–1923
Frankfort—1922
Franklin—1902–1934
Franklin Truck—1907
Frantz—1902
Frayer—1904
Frayer-Miller—1904
Frazer—1946–1951
Fredonia—1902–1904
Fredrickson—1914
Freeman—1901
Freeman—1931
Freemont—1923*
French—1913
Freighter—1917
Friedberg—1908
Friedman—1900–1903
Friedman—1903
Friend—1920–1923
Frisbee—1921
Fritchle Electric—1907–1922
Front-Away—1917*
Frontenac—1908
Frontenac—1917–1922
Frontenac—1922
Front Drive—1921
Frontmobile—1917–1919
F.R.P.—1912
F.S.—1912

Fuller—1908–1911
Fuller—1909
Fuller—1911
Fulton—1908–1909
Fulton—1917
F.W.D. Car—1910
F.W.D. Truck—1910
Fwick—1912

# G

Gabriel— 1912
Gadabout—1914–1916
Gaeth—1898
Gaeth—1904–1911
Gale— 1904
Galt—1914
Gardner—1919–1931
Garford—1907–1908
Garford Truck—1902
Garoscope—1917
Gary—1915*
Gary Truck—1917
Gas-Au-Lec—1905
Gas-Au-Lec—1906
Gas Engine—1905–1906
Gasmobile—1900–1902
Gasoline Motor Carriage—1897
Gatts Horseless Carriage—1905
Gawley—1895
Gay—1915
Gaylord—1911–1914
Gearless—1907–1909
Gearless—1921–1923
Gearless Steamer—1919–1922
Gem—1917–1918
General—1903–1904
General—1912

*Only year produced

General Cab—1929
General Electric—1898–1901
General Vehicle—1906–1919
Genesse—1911–1912
Geneva—1901–1903
Geneva—1911
Geneva—1917*
Gerlinger—1917
German-American—1902
Geronimo—1918–1921
Gersix—1915
Ghent—1917–1918
Giant Truck—1915
Gibbs—1903–1905
Gibson—1899
Gifford-Pettit—1907–1908
Gillette—1916
G.J.G. (George John Grossman)—
    1909–1915
Gleason—1910–1915
Gleason—1914
Glide—1901–1920
Globe—1917
Globe—1921*
Glover—1911
Glover—1921
G.M.C. Truck—1912 to date
Goethemobile—1902
Golden Eagle—1906
Golden Slate—1902
Golden State—1928
Golden West—1919
Goodspeed—1922
Goodwin—1923
Gopher—1911
Gotfredson Truck—1921
Gove—1921

Grabowsky—1908–1913
Graham—1903
Graham—1930–1941
Graham-Fox—1903
Graham-Paige—1927
Gramm—1901
Gramm Truck—1911
Gramm-Bernstein—1912
Gramm-Logan—1908–1910
Grand—1912
Grand Prix (Pontiac)—1962 to
    date
Grand Rapids—1913
Granite Falls—1912
Grant—1913–1922
Grant-Ferris—1901*
Grass-Premier—1923
Graves-Condon—1899
Gray—1916
Gray—1922–1926
Gray-Dort—1917
Great—1903
Great-Arrow—1903
Great Eagle—1911
Great Smith—1907–1912
Great Southern—1911–1914
Great Western—1908–1916
Great Western—1912
Greeley—1903
Green Bay Steamer—1877
Greenleaf—1902
Greenville—1925
Gregory Front Drive—1922
Gregory—1922
Gregory—1948
Grensfelder—1901*
Greuter—1899

*Only year produced

Greyhound—1921–1923
Greyhound—1929
Gride—1903
Grinnell—1910–1915
Griswold—1907
Grout—1898–1914
Grout-Steamer—1906
Guilder Truck—1922
Gurley—1901*
Guy-Vaughan—1912
G.W.W.—1919
Gyroscope—1908

# H

Haase—1904
Hackett—1915–1920
Hackley—1905–1906
Hahn Truck—1914
H.A.L.—1916–1918
Hale—1917
Hal-Fur—1919
Hall—1903–1904
Hall—1915*
Hall—1917*
Hall Gasoline Trap—1895
Halladay—1907–1915
Halladay—1919
Halladay—1920
Halsey—1901–1909
Halton—1901*
Hambrick—1908
Hamilton—1917–1922
Hamely—1903
Hamlin-Holmes—1921*
Hammer—1905–1906
Hammer-Sommer—1903–1904
Handley—1923

Handley-Knight—1921–1923
Hanger—1915
Hannay Truck—1917*
Hanover—1921–1923
Hansen—1902
Hanson—1918–1923
Harberer—1910–1913
Harder—1911
Harding—1911
Hardy—1903
Hare—1918
Harper—1907*
Harrie—1925
Harrigan—1922*
Harris—1893
Harris—1898
Harris Six—1923
Harrisburg—1922
Harrison—1906–1907
Harrison—1912
Harroun—1916–1921
Hart-Kraft—1908
Hartley—1898
Hartman—1898*
Harvard—1915–1922
Harvey—1914
Hasbrouck—1899–1901
Haseltine—1916
Hassler—1917*
Hatfield—1906–1908
Hatfield—1908
Hatfield—1916–1924
Hatfield—1921–1924
Hathaway—1924
Haupt—1909
Haven—1917
Havers—1911–1914

*Only year produced

Haviland—1895
Havoc (Rochester)—1914
Hawk—1914*
Hawk (Studebaker-Packard)—
    1955–1966†
Hawkeye—1917
Hawkeye—1923
Hawkins—1915
Hawley—1907*
Hay-Berg—1907–1908
Haydock—1907–1910
Hayes-Anderson—1928
Haynes—1894–1924
Haynes—1901
Haynes-Apperson—1895
Hayward—1913
Hazard—1914
H.C.S.-Stutz—1920–1926
Healey—1951
Healy Electric—1911*
Hebb—1918
Heifner—1921
Heilman—1908
Heine-Velox—1906–1908
Hendel—1904
Henderson—1912–1914
Hendrickson Truck—1916
Henley—1899
Henney Hearse—1922
Hennigan—1908–1909
Henrietta—1901
Henry—1911–1912
Henry J—1950–1954
Henrylee—1912
Hercules—1914
Hercules Electric—1902

Herff-Brooks—1914–1916
Herreshoff—1909–1915
Herreshoff-Detroit—1914
Herschmann—1904
Hertel—1895–1901
Hertz—1926
Hesseltine—1917
Hess Steam—1902
Hewitt—1905–1913
Hewitt-Lindstrom—1900*
Heymann—1898
Hickenhull—1904
Hicks—1900
Higdon & Higdon Horseless Carriage—1896
Highlander—1922
Highway Knight—1920
Higrade—1919
Hill—1907–1908
Hill's Locomotor—1895
Hillsdale—1908*
Hilton—1908*
Hinde & Dauch—1906–1908
Hines—1908*
Hinkel—1925
Hobbie—1909–1910
Hodge Steamer Fire Engine—1840
Hodgson—1902
Hoffman—1913
Hoffman Gas—1901
Hoffman Steam—1902–1904
Holden—1915
Holland Steam—1905
Holley—1900–1902
Holley—1902
Hollier—1916–1920

*Only year produced
†U.S. production terminated December 1963

Holly—1910–1917
Holmes—1908
Holmes—1918–1922
Holmes Gastricycle—1895
Holsman-Autobuggy—1902–1910
Hol-Tan—1906
Holton—1921
Holtzer-Cabot—1895
Holyoke—1903
Holyoke-Steam—1899–1903
Homer—1908
Homer-Laughlin—1916
Hoosier Scout—1914
Hoover—1917
Hopkins—1902
Hoppenstand—1948
Horner—1917
Horsey Horseless Carriage—1899*
Hoskins—1921
Houghton—1916*
Houghton Steamer—1900–1901
Houk—1917
Houpt—1909
Houpt-Rockwell—1910
House—1920
House-Steamer—1901
Howard—1901
Howard—1903–1906
Howard—1913–1917
Howard Gasoline Wagon—1895
Howe—1907
Howey—1903
H.R.L.—1921
Huber—1894
Hudson—1909–1957
Hudson Steam—1904*
Hudson Steam Car—1901

Huebner—1914
Huffman—1920–1926
Hug Truck—1922
Hughes—1899
Hunt—1905
Hunter—1921
Huntington-Buckboard—1889
Huntington—1907*
Hupmobile—1908–1941
Hupp-Yeats—1911–1919
Hurlburt—1922
Huron—1921
Hurryton—1922
Huselton—1914
Hustler Power Car—1911
Hydro-Car—1901
Hydromotor—1917
Hylander—1922

# I

Ideal—1902
Ideal—1903–1909
Ideal—1905
Ideal—1908–1909
Ideal—1912*
Ideal—1914
Ideal Electric—1910–1911
I.H.C.—1907–1908
Illinois Electric—1901
Illinois Electric—1909–1914
Imp—1913
Imp—1915
Imperial—1900
Imperial—1903–1905
Imperial—1907–1908
Imperial—1912–1916
Imperial—1916*

*Only year produced

223

Imperial (Chrysler)—1926 to date
Independence—1912
Independent—1915-1916
Independent—1920
Independent—1927
Indiana—1910
Indiana—1921
Indiana Truck—1909
Indianapolis—1899
Ingersoll-Rand—1921*
Ingrame-Hatch—1917-1918
Inland—1920
Innes—1921
International-Auto Wagon—1900*
International—1948
International Harvester-Auto Buggy—1907-1912
International Harvester—1907 to date
International Truck—1901
Inter-State—1908-1919
Intrepid—1904
Iowa—1908-1909
Iowa—1919
Iroquois-Buffalo—1906-1908
Iroquois-Seneca—1905-1908
Irvin—1902
Irvington Izzer—1910
Iverson—1908

# J

Jackson—1899
Jackson—1902-1923
Jackson—1920
Jacks Runabout—1900
Jacquet Flyer—1921
James—1911

Janney—1906-1907
Jarvis-Huntington—1912*
Jarvis Truck—1906
Jaxon—1903
Jay—1907-1909
Jay-Eye-See—1921
Jeannin—1908-1909
Jeep—1941 to date
Jeffery—1902-1916
Jeffery—1914
Jem Special—1922
Jenkins—1901
Jenkins—1907-1915
Jersey City—1919
Jetmobile (3 wheel)—1952*
Jewel—1911*
Jewell—1906-1909
Jewett—1906
Jewett—1922-1927
Joerns—1911
Johnson—1905-1912
Johnson—1913*
Johnson Steamer—1901
Joliet—1912
Joly & Lambert—1916*
Jones—1916-1920
Jones-Corbin—1902-1907
Jones Steam Car—1898
Jonz—1909-1912
Jonz-Kansas City—1911
Jonz-New Albany, Ind.—1911
Jordan—1916-1932
J.P.L.—1914
Juergens—1908
Jules—1911
Julian—1925
Julian-Brown—1925

*Only year produced

Jumgo—1918
Junior—1925
Juno Truck—1911
Junz—1902
Juvenile—1906–1907

# K

Kadix—1913
Kaiser—1946–1955
Kaiser Darrin—1952–1954
Kalamazoo—1914
Kalamazoo—1922
Kane-Pennington—1894
Kankakee—1919
Kansas City—1905–1907
Karavan Truck—1920–1922
Karbach—1908–1909
Kardell—1918
Kato—1907
Kauffman—1909–1910
Kavan—1905
Kaws—1922
K.D.—1914
Kearns—1908–1917
Kearns—1916
Keasler—1922*
Keene—1900–1902
Keeton—1908*
Keldon—1920
Keller Cyclecar—1915*
Keller—1947–1949
Keller-Kar—1914
Kelley-Springfield—1918
Kellogg—1903
Kelly—1911
Kelsey—1902
Kelsey—1922–1924

Kelsey & Tilney—1899
Kelsey Friction—1921–1924
Kelsey Motorette—1910–1913
Kendle—1912
Kenilworth—1923
Kenmore—1909–1912
Kennedy—1898
Kennedy—1911
Kensington—1899–1903
Kensington Steam—1908
Kent—1916–1917
Kentucky—1915–1924
Kenworth Truck—1923
Kenworthy—1920–1922
Kermoth—1908*
Kermet—1900*
Kerns—1914
Kerosene Surrey—1900
Kessler—1921
Keystone—1900*
Keystone—1910*
Keystone—1918–1919
Keystone-Motorette—1896
Keystone Steamer—1909
Kiblinger—1907–1909
Kidder—1901*
Kidney—1910*
Kimball Electric—1912*
Kimball—1922
King—1896*
King—1909
King—1911–1924
King Midget—1949
King-Remick—1906
Kingston—1907–1908
King Zeitler—1919
Kinnear—1913

*Only year produced

225

Kinney—1922
Kirk—1903–1905
Kirkham—1906*
Kissel—1906–1931
Kleiber Truck—1910
Klemm—1917
Kline—1909–1923
Kline-Kar—1916
Kling—1907
Klink—1907–1909
Klock—1900*
Klondike—1918
Knickerbocker—1901
Knickerbocker—1912
Knight & Kilbourne—1906–1909
Knight Special—1917
Know—1900
Knox—1900–1915
Knox Truck—1904–1907
Knox—1922
Knox-Landsen—1904
Knudson—1899*
K.O.—1921
Kobusch—1906*
Koehler—1910–1912
Koehler—1919
Komet—1911
Konigslow—1903–1904
Kopp—1911
Koppin—1914
Kraft Steam—1901
Kramer—1915
Krastin—1902–1903
Krebs—1913
Krebs Truck—1922
Kreuger—1904
K-R-I-T—1909–1912

Kron—1915
Kuhn—1918
Kunz—1902–1905
Kurtis—1954
Kurtis-Kraft—1949–1955 (now makes racers)
Kurtz—1921–1926

**L**

Laconia—1900
Lad's Car—1914
LaFayette—1920–1924
LaFayette (Nash)—1934–1939
La France—1910
La France-Republic—1925
La Marne—1920–1921
La Marne Jr.—1919*
Lambert—1891
Lambert—1904
Lambert—1908
Lamphen—1904*
Lamson—1917
Lampher—1909
Lancamobile—1899
Lancaster—1900–1901
Lancer (Dodge)—1960 to date
Landover—1917–1918
Landshaft—1913
Lane—1920
Lane Steamer—1899–1911
Langan—1898
Lange Truck—1921
Langer—1896
Lansden—1904–1910
La Petite—1905
Larchmont—1900

*Only year produced

Lark (Studebaker-Packard)—
   1958–1966†
Larre-Bee-Deyo—1920
Larsen—1908*
Larson—1910
La Salle—1927–1940
LaSalle Niagara—1906*
Lasky—1916
Laughlin—1916–1918
Laurel—1916–1921
Lauth-Juergens—1907–1909
Lavigne—1914
Law—1902
Law—1912
Lawson—1900
Lawter—1909
L.C.E.—1914
L & E—1922
Leach—1899*
Leach-Biltwell—1920–1923
Leader—1911
Lear—1903–1909
Lear—1908–1909
Leganon—1906–1907
Lebgett—1903
Lee Diamond—1911*
Lehigh—1926
Lehr—1908
Le Moon Truck—1917
Lenawee—1900
Lende—1908–1909
Lengert—1896
Lennon—1909*
Lenot—1912–1922
Lenox—1911
Lenox Electric—1908

Leon Mendel—1890
Leon Rubay—1923
Leslie—1918
Lesperance—1911*
Lethbridge—1907
Lever—1930
Lewis—1898
Lewis—1901*
Lewis (6)—1913–1916
Lewis Airmobile—1937
Lexington—1909–1926
Lexington—1914
Liberty—1916–1923
Liberty—1926
Liberty-Brush—1912
Light—1914
Lima—1915
Limited—1911
Lincoln—1908*
Lincoln—1910
Lincoln—1911
Lincoln—1914
Lincoln—1922 to date
Lincoln Continental—1939–1948;
   1957 to date
Lincoln (Leland)—1920–1921
Lincoln Truck—1917
Lincoln Zephyr—1935–1942
Lindsley—1908
Linn—1929
Linscott—1916*
Lion—1910–1912
Lippard—1912
Little—1911–1913
Little—1914
Little—1921

*Only year produced
†U. S. production terminated December 1963

Little Giant Truck—1910
Littlemac—1930
L.M.C.—1919
Locke Steamer—1902
Locomobile—1902–1930
Locomobile Steamer—1899
Logan—1905–1908
Logan—1906
Lomax—1913
Lomgard—1921
London—1922
Lone Star—1920–1923
Long—1875
Long—1923*
Long Distance—1900
Longest—1912
Loomis—1896
Loomis—1901–1904
Lord—1913–1914
Lorraine—1907–1908
Lorraine—1920–1921
Los Angeles—1913
Louisiana—1900
Lowell—1917
Lowell-American—1908–1909
Loyal—1920
Lozier—1901–1918
Lozier Steamer—1901
Lozier-Steamer—1912
L.P.C.—1914–1916
Luck Utility—1913
Ludlow—1915*
Luedinghaus-Espenschied—1919
Luitwieler—1909
Lutz—1917
Luverne—1906–1917
Luxor Cab—1920–1926

Lyman—1904*
Lyman—1909
Lyman & Burnham—1903–1904
Lyon—1911
Lyons-Atlas—1914–1915
Lyons-Knight—1914

# M

Maccar—1914
MacDonald—1920–1923
Mack—1900 to date
Mack Truck—1905
Mackenzie—1914
Mackle-Thompson—1903*
MacNaughton—1907*
Macomber—1913
Macon—1917*
Macy-Roger—1895
Madison—1915–1921
Madison—1921
Magic—1922
Magnolia—1903
Mahoning—1904–1905
Maibohm—1916–1922
Maine—1915–1918
Mais—1911
Maja—1908
Majestic—1913
Majestic—1917–1918
Majestic—1925
Malcolm—1915*
Malcom-Jones—1914*
Malcomson—1906*
Malden Steam—1902
Malvern—1905
Manexall—1921
Manhattan—1907

*Only year produced

Manhattan—1921
Manistee—1912*
Manluis—1910
Manly—1919
Mann—1895
Mansfield—1919
Mansur—1914
Maple-Leaf—1921
Maplebay—1908
Marathon—1908–1915
Marble-Swift—1903–1905
Marion—1901*
Marion—1904–1918
Marion-Handley—1916
Marion-Overland—1910*
Maritime—1913
Mark-Electric—1897
Marlan—1920
Marlboro—1900*
Marlin (Rambler)—1964–1967
Marmon—1903–1933
Marmon-Herrington—1932
Marmon & Nordyke—1902
Marquette—1912*
Marquette—1929–1930
Marr—1903–1904
Marron—1903
Marsh—1898–1899
Marsh—1905
Marsh—1920–1923
Marshall—1919
Marshall—1920–1921
Martin—1910
Martin—1920
Martin—1926
Martin—1931
Martin—1954

Martin-Wasp—1919–1924
Marvel—1907*
Marwin Truck—1918
Maryland—1908–1910
Maryland Electric—1914*
Mascotte—1911
Mason—1906–1915
Mason—1909
Mason—1922
Mason Steamer—1898
Massachusetts—1901*
Massillon—1909*
Master—1918*
Mather—1901
Matheson—1903–1913
Matheson—1906
Mathews—1907*
Mathewson—1904
Mathis—1930–1931
Matilda—1894
Maumee—1906*
Maxfer—1919
Maxim—1912
Maxim—1920
Maxim—1928
Maxim-Goodridge—1908
Maxim Motortricycle—1895
Maxwell—1904–1925
Maxwell-Briscoe—1904–1912
May—1912
Mayer—1899
Mayer—1913
Mayfair—1925
Maytag—1911
M.B.—1910
McCarron—1929
McCormick—1899

*Only year produced

McCrea—1906–1908
McCue—1909–1910
McCullough—1899
McCurdy—1922
McDonald—1923
McFarland—1910–1928
McGee Steamer—1937
McGill—1922*
McIntyre—1909–1915
McKay Steam—1900
McLaughlin—1911
McLaughlin—1916
McLean—1910
McNabb—1910
Mead—1912
Mearo—1909
Mecca—1915
Mechanics—1925
Med-Bow—1907–1908
Medcraft—1907–1908
Media—1900*
Media—1907*
Meech-Stoddard—1924
Meiselbach—1904–1909
Mel Special—1923
Melbourne—1904*
Menard—1921
Menges—1908*
Menominee—1915
Menominee Truck—1920
Mercedes—1902
Mercer—1909–1925
Mercer—1931
Merchant—1914
Mercu—1909–1929
Mercury—1904*
Mercury—1910

Mercury—1914–1915
Mercury—1916–1918
Mercury—1922
Mercury—1930
Mercury (Ford)—1938 to date
Merit—1920–1923
Merkel—1905–1906
Merz—1914
Messerer—1901*
Metcar—1901
Meteor—1902–1903
Meteor—1908–1909
Meteor—1914
Meteor—1921*
Metropol—1914–1915
Metropolitan—1917
Metropolitan—1922–1923
Metz—1909–1921
Metzcar—1909–1912
Metzger—1909
Meyer—1922
Michelet—1921
Michigan—1903–1907
Michigan—1910–1911
Michigan—1911–1913
Michigan Hearse—1914
Michigan Steamer—1908–1909
Middleby—1908–1912
Midgley—1905
Midland—1908–1913
Midwest Tractor—1918
Mier—1908–1910
Mieusset—1907
Mighty Michigan—1913
Milac—1916
Milburn Electric—1915–1924
Miller—1903*

*Only year produced

230

Miller—1907–1908
Miller—1912–1913
Miller—1921
Miller Special—1907–1908
Mills—1876
Mills Milwaukee—1900
Milwaukee—1925
Milwaukee Steam—1900–1902
Minneapolis—1919
Mino—1914
Mission—1914
Mitchell—1903–1923
Mitchell-Lewis—1903–1917
Mobile—1902
Mobile Steamer (Crane)—1899–
    1903
Mobilette—1913–1915
Mock—1906
Model—1903–1906
Model—1907–1909
Modern—1907–1910
Modern—1912
Modoc—1911
Moehn—1895
Moeller—1911
Mogul—1912
Mohawk—1903–1904
Mohawk—1914
Mohler—1901–1905
Mohler & DeGress—1901–1905
Moligan—1920
Moline—1904–1917
Moline—1911
Moline—1920
Moline-Knight—1913
Moline-Knight—1918
Moller Cab—1920

Monarch—1903–1905
Monarch—1905–1908
Monarch—1907–1909
Monarch—1914–1916
Moncrief—1901
Mondex-Magic—1914
Monitor—1910*
Monitor—1915
Monroe—1915–1922
Monsen—1908–1909
Moody—1900
Mooers—1900
Moon—1905–1931
Moon—1914
Moore—1902–1903
Moore—1906–1907
Moore—1916–1920
Moorespring Vehicle—1890
Moorespring Vehicle Steam—1888
Mora—1906–1911
Moreland Truck—1911
Morgan—1897
Morgan—1908–1909
Mor-Power—1921
Morlock—1903
Morris-London—1922
Morris Salom Electrobat—1895–
    1897
Morrison Electric—1891
Morrissey—1925
Mors—1901
Mors—1906
Morse—1904
Morse—1909
Morse—1915–1916
Morse Cyclecar—1914–1915
Morse Steam Car—1904–1906

*Only year produced

Mort—1925
Motor Buggy—1908–1910
Motor Truck—1902*
Motorcar—1906–1908
Motorette—1906
Motorette—1911–1913
Motorette—1946
Mountain Road—1917
Mover—1902
Moyea—1903–1904
Moyer—1912–1915
M.P.C.—1925
M & P Electric—1912–1913
M.P.M.—1915
Mt. Pleasant—1914–1916
Mueller—1896
Mueller-Benz—1895
Mueller-Trap—1901
Mulford—1909
Multiplex—1913
Munch Allen—1910*
Muncie—1903
Muncie—1906
Munsing—1908*
Munsing—1913
Munson—1900
Muntz Jet—1951
Murdaugh—1900*
Murray—1901
Murray—1916–1920
Murray-Max Six—1921–1926
Muskegon—1918
Mustang—1948
Mustang (Ford)—1964 to date
Mutual—1914–1918
Mutual—1919

Myer B. & F.—1912
Myers—1904

## N

Nadig—1889
Nance—1911–1912
Napier (of America)—1904–1912
Napoleon—1916–1917
Napoleon—1918
Narragansett—1915
National—1903–1906
Nash—1917–1957
Nash Healy—1951–1954
Natco—1912
National—1900–1924
National—1903–1906
National—1923
National Electric—1900
National Sextet—1920
Nebraska—1926
Neilson—1907*
Nelson—1905
Nelson—1917–1920
Nelson-Brennen Peterson—1914–1915
Nelson and Le Moon—1915–1920
Netco Truck—1916
Neustadt-Perry—1903
Neustadt—1912
Nevada—1908*
Nevada Truck—1913–1915
Nevin—1927
Newark—1912
Newcomb—1921
New Departure—1909–1910
New England Truck—1914

*Only year produced

New Era—1902
New Era—1916
New Era—1929–1931
New Haven—1899
New Haven—1911
New Home—1901
New Orleans—1920
New Perry—1903
Newport—1916
New Way—1907
New York—1900*
New York—1907*
New York—1926
Niagara—1903
Niagara—1915
Nichols-Shepard—1912
Niles—1916
Niles—1921
Noble Truck—1917
Nolan—1924
Noma—1919–1923
Nonpareil—1913*
Northern—1903–1908
Northway—1921
Northwestern—1904*
Norton—1901–1902
Norwalk—1912–1922
Novara—1917
Nucar—1929
Nyberg—1912–1914

## O

Oakland—1907–1931
Oakman—1898–1900
Obertine—1915
O.B. Truck—1928
O'Connell—1928

Odelot—1916
Offenhauser—1934
Ogden Truck—1918
Ogren—1907
Ogren—1915–1920
Ohio (Packard)—1899–1902
Ohio—1909–1918
Ohio—1914
Ohio—1915
Ohio Electric—1900–1915
Ohio Falls—1911–1915
Okay—1907
Okey—1903–1908
O.K. Truck—1917
O.K. Truck—1925
Oldfield—1917
Old Hickory—1915
Old Reliable—1912
Old Reliable—1926
Oldsmobile—1896 to date
Olds Steam Car—1896
Oliver—1911
Oliver—1935
Olympian—1917–1920
Olympic—1913
Olympic—1922
Omar—1908–1910
Omaha—1912
Omort—1927
Oneida Truck—1917
Only—1909–1911
Only Car—1911–1915
Oregon—1916
Orient—1900
Orient-Auto-Go—1900
Oriole—1927
Orion—1900*

*Only year produced

233

Orleans—1920
Orlo—1904
Ormond—1904
Orson—1911
Oscarlear—1905
Oshkosh—1926
Oshkosh Steamer—1877
Oshkosh Truck—1917
Otto—1909
Ottokar—1903
Otto-Mobile—1911–1912
Overholt Steam—1912
Overland—1903*
Overland—1906–1909
Overman—1899–1902
O-We-Go—1914
Owen—1899
Owen—1910
Owen Magnetic—1915–1920
Owen-Schoenieck—1915
Owen-Thomas—1908
Owosso—1911
Oxford—1905

# P

Pacific—1914
Pacific Special—1911
Packard—1899–1958
Packers—1911
Packet—1915
Packet—1917
Page—1907*
Page—1908–1909
Page—1923
Page-Toledo—1910
Paige—1910
Paige-Detroit—1909–1928

Pak-Age-Car—1925
Palace—1912*
Palmer—1906*
Palmer—1912
Palmer-Moore—1905
Palmer-Singer—1907–1920
Pan—1918–1920
Pan-American—1902–1904
Pan-American—1917–1921
Panda—1954
Panhard Truck—1917–1918
Panther—1908
Paragon—1906
Paragon—1917
Paragon—1922*
Paramount Cab—1924
Parenth—1921
Parenti—1920–1921
Parker—1919
Parker—1922
Parkin—1903–1909
Parry—1911*
Parsons—1906*
Partin—1913
Partin-Palmer—1913–1917
Pasco—1908
Pastora—1913*
Paterson—1908–1924
Pathfinder—1911–1918
Patrician—1917
Patriot—1922
Patterson-Greenfield—1916
Pawtucket—1901–1902
Payne-Modern—1906
Peabody—1907
Peck—1897
Peerless—1900–1932

*Only year produced

Peerles Steam—1902–1909
Peet—1923–1926
Peets—1908*
Pelletier—1906*
Penford—1924
Peninsular—1915
Penn—1911–1913
Penn-Unit—1911*
Pennant—1923
Pennington—1890
Pennington—1894
Pennsy—1917
Pennsy—1918
Pennsylvania—1907–1913
Pennsylvania—1916–1917
People's—1901*
Perego-Clarkston Truck—1920
Perfection—1906–1908
Perfex—1912
Perry—1895
Peru—1938
P.E.T.—1913
Peter Pan—1907
Peter Pan—1914
Peters—1921–1924
Petrel—1908–1912
Phelps—1903–1905
Phianna—1917–1920
Phianna—1919
Philadelphia—1924
Philion—1892
Phipps—1911–1912
Phipps-Johnston—1909*
Phoenix—1900
Pickard—1908–1912
Pickwick—1930
Piedmont—1918–1920

Pierce—1903
Pierce-Arrow—1901–1938
Pierce Motorette—1901*
Pierce-Racine—1903–1911
Pierce-Stanhope—1903
Piggins—1909–1910
Piggins—1912
Pilgrim—1916–1918
Pilliod—1916
Pilot—1911–1923
Pioneer—1909–1911
Pioneer—1914–1915
Pioneer—1917
Pioneer—1920
Pirate—1907
Pirsch—1910
Piscorski—1901
Pitcher—1920
Pittsburgh—1896–1899
Pittsburgh—1905–1909
Pittsburgh—1905–1908
Pittsburgh—1908–1911
Pittsburgh Electric—1905–1911
Pittsburgher—1919
Pittsfield—1907*
Planche—1906
Plass Motor Sleigh—1895
Playboy—1946–1949
Plymouth—1908–1910
Plymouth—1928 to date
Plymouth Truck—1908
P.M.C. Buggyabout—1908—
    N.Y.C.
Pneumobile—1914–1915
Pokorney—1905
Polo—1927
Pomaroy—1902*

*Only year produced

Ponder—1916
Ponder—1922
Pontiac—1906–1909
Pontiac—1908*
Pontiac—1926 to date
Pope—1895–1899
Pope Columbia—1897
Pope-Hartford—1897–1914
Pope Motor—1903–1908
Pope-Robinson—1902–1904
Pope-Toledo—1901–1909
Pope-Tribune—1902–1909
Pope-Waverly—1903–1908
Poppy Car—1917
Porter—1900
Porter—1920–1922
Port Huron—1918
Portland—1914
Poss—1912
Postal—1907–1908
Powell—1912
Powercar—1909–1911
Poyer—1913
Practical—1906–1909
Prado—1921
Pratt—1911–1916
Praul—1895
Preferred—1920
Premier—1903–1926
Premocar—1920
Prescott—1901–1905
Preston—1921–1923
Pridemore—1914
Prigg—1915
Primo—1906
Primo—1911*
Prince—1902

Princess—1905
Princess—1914–1918
Princess—1917
Princeton—1923
Progress—1912
Prospect—1902
Prudence—1912
Pullman—1907–1908
Publix—1946
Pungs-Finch—1904–1910
Pup—1948
Puritan Stream—1902
Pyramid—1902

## Q

Quakertown—1915*
Queen—1902–1906
Quick—1899
Quinlan—1904*
Quinsley—1904

## R

R & L Electric—1920
R.A.C.—1911–1912
Racine—1895
Rae—1909
Rae Electric—1898
Railsbach—1914
Rainier—1905–1911
Ralco—1904
Raleigh—1920
Rambler—1900
Rambler—1902–1913
Rambler (Nash)—1950
Rambler—1957 to date
Rambler-American—1958 to date
Randall—1903–1906

*Only year produced

Randall Steamer—1902–1903
Randolph Steam—1908–1910
Ranger—1907*
Ranger—1910–1911
Ranger—1921–1922
Ranier—1911
Rapid Truck—1902–1913
Rassel—1911
Rassler—1907
Rauch & Lang—1905–1915
Rauch & Lang Electric—1920–1924
Rayfield—1911–1915
R.C.H.—1911–1914
Read—1913–1914
Reading—1912–1918
Reading Steamer—1960
Real—1915
Reber—1902–1903
Red Bug—1928
Red Arrow—1915–1916
Red Ball—1924
Red Devil Steamer—1866
Red Jacket—1907
Redshield—1911*
Red Wing—1928
Reed—1909
Rees—1921
Reeves—1897
Reeves—1908–1909
Reeves (Sexto Auto)—1910
Reeves (Octo Auto)—1911
Regal—1908–1918
Regas—1903–1905
Regent—1917
Rehberger Truck—1924
Reid—1903–1905

Reiland & Bree—1928
Reinertsen—1902
Relay Truck—1921
Reliable—1906–1909
Reliable-Dayton—1908–1909
Reliance—1903–1909
Reliance—1917
Remel-Vincent Steam—1923
Remington—1901–1904
Remington—1912
Remington—1915–1916
Rennoc—1918
Reno—1908
Renville—1911
Reo—1904–1936
Reo Truck—1908 to date
Republic—1912–1913
Republic Truck—1914–1931
Revere—1918–1926
Rex—1914–1915
Reya—1918
Reynolds—1920
Rhodes—1908
Richard—1917–1918
Richards—1914
Richelieu—1922–1923
Richmond—1908–1912
Richmond—1915
Rickenbacker—1922–1927
Ricketts—1902
Ricketts Diamond—1909*
Rickmobile—1948
Riddle—1916
Riddle—1922–1924
Rider-Lewis—1908–1909
Riess-Royal—1922
Rigs-That-Run—1899

*Only year produced

237

Riker Electric Stanhope—1896–1901
Riker Gasoline—1900
Riley & Cowley—1902
Rinker Electric—1898
Riper—1917
Ritz—1915–1916
Riveria—1907
Riviera (Buick)—1962 to date
R.M.C.—1908
R.O.—1911
Roadable—1946*
Roader—1911–1912
Road Cart (R. S. Scott)—1896
Road King—1922
Road Plane—1945
Roadster—1903
Roadster—1915
Roamer—1916–1925
Robe—1923*
Roberts—1904*
Roberts Six—1921
Robie—1914
Robinson—1900–1902
Robinson—1914
Robson—1908–1909
Robson—1908–1911
Roche—1920–1926
Rochester—1901
Rockaway—1904
Rockcliff—1905
Rocket—1913
Rocket—1924
Rockette—1946
Rock Falls—1920
Rockford—1908
Rock Hill—1916

Rockne—1931–1933
Rockwell—1908
Rodgers—1903–1905
Rodgers—1921
Roebling—1909*
Roger—1903*
Rogers—1895
Rogers—1911–1912
Rogers Steamer—1899
Rogers & Hanford—1901–1902
Rollin—1923–1925
Rolls-Royce (U.S.)—1920–1931
Roman—1909
Romer—1921–1924
Roosevelt—1929–1931
Root and Van Dervoort—1904*
Roper-Steamer—1865
Roper Steam Vehicle—1894
Ross—1905–1909
Ross—1915–1918
Ross—1929
Rossler—1907*
Rotarian—1921
Rotary—1904–1905
Rotary—1916–1917
Rotary—1922
Rovan—1914
Rovena-Front Drive—1926
Rowe—1911
Rowe-Stuart—1922
Royal—1904*
Royal—1914
Royal Electric—1905*
Royal Tourist—1904–1912
Rubay—1922–1924
Rugby Truck—1927
Ruggles—1905*

*Only year produced

Ruggles Truck—1921
Ruler—1917
Rumley—1920
Runabout—1902
Runner—1913*
Rush—1918
Rushmobile—1902*
Russell—1902
Russell—1903*
Russell—1910
Russell-Knight—1914
Rutenber—1903
Ruxton—1929–1931
R & V Knight—1919–1924
Ryder—1908–1911
Rylander—1914*

## S

Safety—1909
Safety—1917
Sateway—1925
Saf-T-Cab—1926
Saginaw—1916–1917
Salisbury Motorcycle—1895
Salter—1909
Salvador—1914–1915
Sampson—1904–1911
Sampson—1919
Sampson Electric Truck—1907
Samson—1919–1923
Sanbert—1911
Sandow Cab—1925
Sandow Truck—1915
Sanford-Herbert—1911
Sanford Truck—1918
Sandusky—1903–1904
Sandusky—1911

Santos Dumont—1903
Savage—1912
Sawyer—1913
Saxon—1914–1922
Saxon-Duplex—1920
Sayer—1917
Sayers & Scoville—1907–1924
Scarad—1946
Schact—1905–1913
Schaefer—1910*
Schaum—1901*
Schebler—1908
Schleicher—1895
Schloemer—1889
Schlosser—1912
Schlotterback—1912
Schmidt—1910
Schnader—1907*
Schnader—1914–1918
Schoeneck—1917
Schoening—1895
Schwartz—1920
Scientific—1921
Scioto—1911
Scootmobile—1947
Scott—1921
Scott-Newcomb Steam—1921
Scout (International Harvester)—
    1961 to date
Scripps—1911
Scripps-Booth—1914–1922
Scripps-Booth Cyclecar—1914*
Seagrave—1912
Seagrave—1921
Searchmont—1900–1903
Sears—1908–1909
Sears Motor Buggy—1908–1909

*Only year produced

239

Sebring—1909–1912
Seitz—1911
Sekine—1923
Selden—1906–1914
Selden Truck—1913
Sellers—1909
Sellew-Royce—1909
Seminole—1928
Senator—1906–1911
Seneca—1917–1924
Serpentina—1915
Serrifile—1921
Service Truck—1919
Servitor—1907
Seven-Little-Buffaloes—1908
Severin—1920–1922
S. G. Gay—1915
S. G. V.—1910–1915
Sha—1920
Shadburn—1917–1918
Shad-Wyck—1917
Shain—1902–1903
Shamrock—1917
Sharon—1915
Sharp—1915
Sharp-Arrow—1909–1911
Shaum—1905–1908
Shavers Steam Buggy—1895
Shaw—1900
Shaw—1914–1920
Shaw—1921
Shawmut—1905
Shelby—1902–1903
Shelby—1917
Shelby GT (Shelby American)—
   1965 to date
Sheldon—1905

Sheridan—1921*
Shoemaker—1908–1909
Sibley—1911*
Sibley-Curtis—1912
Siebert—1907–1909
Sigma—1914
Signal—1915
Signet—1913
Silent—1906
Silent Knight—1912
Silent Souix—1910
Silver Knight—1906
Simmons—1910
Simms—1920
Simonds Steam Wagon—1895
Simplex—1905–1919
Simplex-Crane—1915
Simplicity—1907–1911
Simplo—1908
Sinclair—1921
Sinclair-Scott—1906–1907
Singer—1916
Single Center—1908–1910
Sintz—1903–1904
Six-Wheel Truck—1921
Sizer—1911
S.J.R.—1915–1916
Skelton—1920–1923
Skene—1900–1901
S. & M.—1913
Small—1915
Small—1919–1922
Smith—1905–1911
Smith—1912
Smith & Mabley—1905–1907
Smith Motor Wheel—1909
Smith Spring Motor—1896

*Only year produced

240

S.N.—1921
Snyder—1908–1909
Sommer—1908
Soules—1905–1908
South Bend—1919
Southern—1922
Southern—1908–1910
Southern Six—1921–1922
Sovereign—1907
Spacke—1919
Spartan—1907
Spaulding—1902–1903
Spaulding—1911–1916
Special—1906
Special (Buick)—1960 to date
Specialty—1898
Speed Wagon—1918
Speedway—1904
Speedway Special—1918
Speedwell—1907–1915
Spencer—1914*
Spencer—1921
Spencer Steamer—1862
Spencer Steamer—1901
Spenny—1915*
Sperling—1921
Sperry—1903
Sphinx—1914–1916
Spicer—1903
Spiller—1900*
Spillman—1907
Spoerer—1909–1914
Sport—1921
Sportsman (Cord)—1965–1966
Spracke—1921
Sprague—1896
Springer—1904–1906

Springfield—1900–1901
Springfield—1901*
Springfield—1903–1904
Springfield—1909–1910
Sprite—1914
Squier Steam—1899
S & S Hearse—1907
S.S.E.—1917
Stafford—1911–1915
Stahl—1910
Stanmobile—1901
Standard—1902*
Standard—1903–1905
Standard—1909
Standard—1916–1923
Standard Electric—1911–1914
Standard Eight—1917
Standard Electrique—1903
Standard Six—1910–1911
Standard Steamer—1900
Stanhope—1903
Stanhope—1905
Stanley—1903*
Stanley Steamer—1897–1924
Stanley-Whitney—1899–1902
Stanton-Steam—1901
Stanwood—1920–1922
Star—1904
Star—1914
Star—1917
Star—1922–1931
Starbuck—1914
Star-Flee Truck—1927
Starin—1903
States—1915–1916
States—1918
Static—1923

*Only year produced

Staver—1907-1914
Steamobile—1901-1902
Steam Vehicle—1900-1903
Stearns—1898-1929
Stearns-Electric—1900-1904
Stearns-Knight—1911
Stearns Steam Car—1900-1904
Steco—1914
Steele—1915
Steel Swallow—1907-1908
Stegeman—1911
Steinhart-Jensen—1908
Stein-Koenig—1926
Steinmetz—1920
Step-N-Drive—1929
Stephens—1916-1924
Stephenson—1910
Sterling—1909-1911
Sterling—1915*
Sterling—1921-1923
Sterling Knight—1922-1926
Sterkenburg—1931
Sternberg—1909
Stetson—1917
Stevens—1915
Stevens-Duryea—1902-1915
Stevens-Duryea—1919-1924
Stewart—1895
Stewart—1915
Stewart-Coates—1922
Steward Truck—1912
Stickney Motorette—1913
Stilson—1908-1910
St. Cloud—1921
St. Joe—1909*
St. Johns—1903
St. Louis—1899-1907

St. Louis—1899-1900
St. Louis—1922
Stoddard—1911
Stoddard-Dayton—1904*
Stoddard-Knight—1911
Storck—1902
Storms—1915-1916
Stoughton—1919
Stout—1946
Stout Scarab—1935
Strathmore—1900-1901
Stratton—1901-1902
Stratton—1908-1909
Stratton—1908-1909
Stratton—1923*
Streator—1905-1915
Stringer Steam—1901
Strobel & Martin—1910
Strong & Rogers—1900*
Strouse Steam—1915*
Struss—1897
Studebaker Brothers—1902-1912
Studebaker—1912 to date
Studebaker Electric—1902
Studebaker E.M.F.—1909
Studebaker-Garford—1908
Sturgis—1895
Sturges—1898
Sturtevant—1904-1907
Stutz—1912-1934
Stuyvesant—1911-1912
Suburban—1910-1912
Success—1906-1909
Success—1920
Sullivan—1904*
Sullivan Truck—1910
Sultan—1906-1912

*Only year produced

Sultanic—1913
Summit—1907
Sun—1915–1917
Sunset—1906–1907
Super Cooled—1923
Super Kar—1946
Super Truck—1920–1928
Superba (Checker Motors)—1959
Superior—1908
Superior—1918
Super Traction—1923*
Supreme—1917*
Supreme—1922
Supreme—1930
Swanson—1911*
Sweany Steam Carriage—1895
Synnestvedt—1904–1908
Syracuse—1899
Syracuse—1905

## T

Taft Steam—1901
Tait—1923
Tally-Ho—1914
Tarkington—1922
Tarrytown 1914
Tasco—1947
Taylor—1921
Taunton—1901–1902
Taunton—1904*
Teel—1913
Tempest (Pontiac)—1960 to date
Templar—1918–1925
Temple—1899
Templeton-Dubrie—1910
Tennant—1915
Terraplane—1932–1939

Terwilliger Steam—1904
Tex—1915
Texan—1919
Texas—1918–1921
Texmobile—1921
Thermot Monohan—1919
Thomart—1921
Thomas-Detroit—1906–1908
Thomas Flyer—1902–1912
Thomas Truck—1907*
Thompson—1902–1904; 1907–1908
Thomson—1901–1908
Thorne—1929
Thornycroft—1901–1903
Thorobred—1901
Thresher—1900
Thunderbird (Ford)—1954 to date
Tiffany—1913
Tiffin—1914
Tiger—1914
Tiley—1907–1910
Tiley—1904*
Tincher—1904–1909
Tinkham—1899
Titan—1916
Titan—1919
Titan Truck—1917
Titan Vim—1925
Tjaarda—1934
Toledo—1902
Toledo—1909–1910
Toledo—1915
Toledo Steamer—1903
Tonawanda—1900*
Toquet—1905
Torbensen—1906–1908

*Only year produced

243

Toronado (Oldsmobile)—1965 to date
Touraine—1912–1916
Tourist—1903
Tower—1918
Town Car—1909
Town Shopper—1948
Trabold—1921
Tractmobile Steam—1900
Traffic—1914
Transit—1912
Transport Truck—1923
Trask-Detroit—1922
Traveler—1906–1907
Traveler—1910
Traveler—1914–1915
Traveler—1924
Travellall (International Harvester) —1961 to date
Traverse City—1918
Traylor—1920
Trebert—1907*
Triangle—1918
Tribune—1913
Tri-Car—1907
Tricar—1912
Tricolet—1905*
Triple Truck—1909*
Triplex—1905
Tri-Moto—1901
Trinity Steam—1900
Triumph—1900–1901
Triumph—1906–1907
Triumph—1908–1910
Triumph—1911
Triumph—1920
Trojan—1916

Trombly—1911
Troy—1908–1909
Trumbull—1914–1916
Tucker Mobile—1900
Tucker Torpedo—1946
Tudhope—1913
Tulcar—1915
Tulsa—1917–1920
Tulsa—1921
Turnbull—1918
Twin Coach—1927
Twin City—1910
Twombly—1914–1916
Twyford—1902–1908

## U

Ultimate—1920
Ultra—1908–1911
Ultra—1918
Union—1902–1905
Union Truck—1902–1904
Union—1908–1909
Union—1912
Union—1917
United Motor—1902
United—1902–1904
United—1916
Unito—1908
Universal—1912
Universal—1917
Universal—1919
University—1907*
Unwin—1907
Upton—1903–1905
Upton—1904–1906
Urgan—1913
U.S.—1908

*Only year produced

U.S. Auto—1899–1918
U.S. Carriage—1910–1918
U.S. Long Distance—1900–1904
U.S. Motor Car—1908*
U.S. Motor Vehicle—1899–1901
Utility—1910
Utility—1918

# V

Valiant (Chrysler)—1959 to date
Valley Dispatch—1927
Van—1904
Van Auken—1914
Van Dyke—1912
Van L.—1911
Vandergrift—1907*
Vandewater—1908–1914
Vanell Steam Carriage—1895
Van Wagoner—1900
Vaughn—1905*
Vaughn—1913–1914
Vaughn—1923
V.E.C.—1903
Veerac—1911
Velie—1908–1929
Vernon—1916–1920
Verrett Motor Wagon—1896
Versare—1928
Vestal—1914
Veteran—1921
Viall—1917
Victor—1906–1913
Victor—1907–1909
Victor—1908–1911
Victor—1913–1915
Victor—1921
Victors—1923

Victor Steamer—1900
Victoria—1900
Victory—1920
Viking—1908
Viking—1929–1930
Vim Cyclecar—1915
Vim Truck—1914
Virginian—1911
Vixen Cyclecar—1914–1916
Vogel—1909*
Vogue—1918–1922
Vogul—1918
Voiturette—1914
Voltra—1917
Voltz—1915
Vreeland—1920
Vulcan—1913–1915
Vulcan—1920

# W

Wachusell Truck—1921
Waco—1915
Wade—1913
Wagenhals—1913
Wagonette—1901
Wagner—1902*
Wahl—1914*
Waldron—1909–1911
Walker—1911
Walker Truck—1905–1906
Walls—1901–1904
Wallworth—1905*
Walter—1904–1909
Walter—1921
Walter Truck—1914
Waltham—1898
Waltham—1900–1909

*Only year produced

245

Waltham—1905
Waltham—1922
Waltham Orient—1901
Walther—1903
Walton—1902
Walworth—1905
Ward—1920
Ward Electric—1914
Ward La France—1919
Ward Leonard—1901–1903
Ware (4 Wheel)—1918
Warner Electric—1895
Warren—1905
Warren—1911
Warren-Detroit—1909–1913
Warwick—1901–1904
Washington—1907–1912
Washington—1921–1923
Wasp—1920
Waterloo—1904–1905
Waterville—1911
Watrous—1905*
Watson—1907
Watson—1916
Watt Steam—1910
Waukesha—1908
Waverly Electric—1898–1917
Wayne—1904–1908
Wayne—1905–1917
Wayne—1916
Webb—1904*
Webberville—1920
Webb-Jay Steam—1908
Weber—1905*
Weeks—1908*
Wege—1917*
Weier-Smith—1917

Welch—1904–1909
Welch-Detroit—1911
Welch and Lawson—1895
Welch-Marquette—1904
Welch-Pontiac—1911
Werner Truck—1926
West Gasoline Vehicle—1895
Westcott—1910–1924
Western—1901–1911
Western—1907*
Westfield Steam—1910
Westinghouse—1901
Westman—1912
Weston—1896
West Steamer—1897
Weyher—1910
W.F.S.—1912*
Whaley-Henriette—1900
Wharton—1921–1923
Wheel—1902
Whippet—1926–1931
Whitcomb—1928
White—1901–1919
White Hall—1911
White Hickory—1906
White Hickory—1917
Whiteside—1911
White Star—1910–1911
White Star—1912
White Truck—1902 to date
Whiting—1905*
Whiting—1906–1907
Whitman—1908–1909
Whitney—1898–1899
Wichita—1912
Wichita Truck—1918
Wick—1902*

*Only year produced

Wilcox—1907–1912
Wilcox Truck—1910–1927
Wildfire—1953
Wildman—1902*
Will Truck—1928*
Willard—1905
Willet—1912
Williams—1907
Willingham—1916
Wills St. Clair—1921
Willys—1930 to date
Willys-Knight—1913
Willys-Overland—1908–1951
Wilson—1903–1905
Wilson Truck—1915
Windsor—1906–1911
Windsor—1929–1930
Winfield—1921
Wing—1896
Wing—1922
Winkler—1911
Winner—1899
Winther—1920–1923
Winther Truck—1917
Winton—1896–1925
Wisco—1910
Wisconsin—1899*
Wisconsin—1910–1911
Wisconsin Truck—1921
Witt Will—1917
Witt Thompson—1921–1923
Wizard—1914
Wizard—1921
Wolfe—1907
Wolverine—1896
Wolverine—1905–1906

Wolverine—1913
Wolverine—1917–1920
Wolverine—1921
Wolverine—1927
Wolverine-Detroit—1912
Wonder—1909*
Wonder—1917
Woodburn—1912
Woodruff—1902
Woods—1899–1919
Woods—1907
Woods—1918
Woods Magnetic—1917
Woods-Mobilette—1907
Wood Truck—1905*
World Truck—1927
Worth—1907–1908
Worthington—1904–1906
Wright—1925
Wyeth—1913*

# X

Xenia—1915

# Y

Yale—1903
Yale—1917
Yale—1921
Yankee—1910
Yankee Cyclecar—1914
Yellow Cab—1921
Yellow Coach—1921
Yellow Knight—1928
York—1904–1910
York-Pullman—1908–1917
Young—1921

*Only year produced

# Z
Zeitler & Lamson—1917
Zent—1906–1907
Zentmobile—1903

Zephyr—1936–1940
Zimmerman—1907–1916
Zip—1913

# highlights

The story of highway transportation in America and its influence on the American people and their way of life can sometimes be most succinctly told in terms of pure facts and figures. These cold numbers in the following tables actually are the highlights of that story.

## Historical Motor Vehicle Statistics

### MOTOR VEHICLE REGISTRATIONS

| Year | Passenger Cars (Thousand) | Buses (Thousand) | Trucks (Thousands) | Total (Thousands) |
|------|------|------|------|------|
| 1900 | 8 | — | — | 8 |
| 1905 | 77 | — | 1 | 79 |
| 1910 | 458 | — | 10 | 469 |
| 1915 | 2,332 | — | 159 | 2,491 |
| 1920 | 8,132 | — | 1,108 | 9,239 |
| 1925 | 17,481 | 18 | 2,570 | 20,069 |
| 1926 | 19,268 | 24 | 2,908 | 22,200 |
| 1927 | 20,193 | 28 | 3,082 | 23,303 |
| 1928 | 21,362 | 32 | 3,294 | 24,689 |
| 1929 | 23,121 | 34 | 3,550 | 26,705 |
| 1930 | 23,035 | 41 | 3,675 | 26,750 |
| 1931 | 22,396 | 42 | 3,656 | 26,094 |
| 1932 | 20,901 | 43 | 3,446 | 24,391 |
| 1933 | 20,657 | 45 | 3,457 | 24,159 |
| 1934 | 21,545 | 52 | 3,665 | 25,262 |
| 1935 | 22,568 | 59 | 3,919 | 26,546 |
| 1936 | 24,183 | 63 | 4,262 | 28,507 |

| 1937 | 25,467 | 83 | 4,509 | 30,059 |
| 1938 | 25,250 | 88 | 4,476 | 29,814 |
| 1939 | 26,226 | 92 | 4,691 | 31,010 |
| 1940 | 27,466 | 101 | 4,886 | 32,453 |
| 1941 | 29,624 | 120 | 5,150 | 34,894 |
| 1942 | 27,973 | 136 | 4,895 | 33,004 |
| 1943 | 26,009 | 152 | 4,727 | 30,888 |
| 1944 | 25,566 | 153 | 4,760 | 30,479 |
| 1945 | 25,797 | 162 | 5,076 | 31,035 |
| 1946 | 28,217 | 174 | 5,982 | 34,373 |
| 1947 | 30,849 | 187 | 6,805 | 37,841 |
| 1948 | 33,355 | 197 | 7,534 | 41,086 |
| 1949 | 36,458 | 209 | 8,023 | 44,690 |
| 1950 | 40,339 | 224 | 8,599 | 49,162 |
| 1951 | 42,688 | 230 | 8,994 | 51,913 |
| 1952 | 43,823 | 240 | 9,199 | 53,262 |
| 1953 | 46,429 | 244 | 9,544 | 56,217 |
| 1954 | 48,468 | 248 | 9,789 | 58,505 |
| 1955 | 52,144 | 255 | 10,289 | 62,689 |
| 1956 | 54,211 | 259 | 10,679 | 65,148 |
| 1957 | 55,918 | 264 | 10,943 | 67,125 |
| 1958 | 56,891 | 270 | 11,136 | 68,297 |
| 1959 | 59,454 | 265 | 11,635 | 71,354 |
| 1960 | 61,682 | 272 | 11,914 | 73,868 |
| 1961 | 63,417 | 280 | 12,261 | 75,958 |
| 1962 | 66,108 | 285 | 12,780 | 79,173 |
| 1963 | 69,055 | 298 | 13,360 | 82,714 |
| 1964 | 71,983 | 305 | 14,013 | 86,301 |
| 1965 | 75,261 | 314 | 14,795 | 90,370 |
| 1966 | 78,331 | 323 | 15,522 | 94,177 |

| Year | Vehicle Miles of Travel (Billions) | Special Motor Vehicle Taxes (Millions) | Highway Expenditures (Millions) |
|---|---|---|---|
| 1925 | 122 | | $ 1,755 |
| 1926 | 141 | | 1,825 |
| 1927 | 158 | | 2,049 |
| 1928 | 173 | | 2,196 |
| 1929 | 198 | | 2,249 |
| 1930 | 206 | $   851 | 2,541 |
| 1931 | 216 | 882 | 2,404 |
| 1932 | 201 | 915 | 1,904 |
| 1933 | 201 | 1,051 | 1,703 |
| 1934 | 216 | 1,119 | 2,020 |

| | | | |
|---|---|---|---|
| 1935 | 229 | 1,212 | 1,773 |
| 1936 | 252 | 1,363 | 2,491 |
| 1937 | 270 | 1,504 | 2,313 |
| 1938 | 271 | 1,445 | 2,675 |
| 1939 | 285 | 1,576 | 2,501 |
| 1940 | 302 | 1,743 | 2,378 |
| 1941 | 334 | 2,041 | 2,155 |
| 1942 | 268 | 1,942 | 1,769 |
| 1943 | 208 | 1,555 | 1,344 |
| 1944 | 213 | 1,613 | 1,349 |
| 1945 | 250 | 1,809 | 1,429 |
| 1946 | 341 | 2,414 | 2,043 |
| 1947 | 371 | 2,891 | 2,866 |
| 1948 | 398 | 3,259 | 3,444 |
| 1949 | 424 | 3,590 | 3,913 |
| 1950 | 458 | 4,094 | 4,155 |
| 1951 | 491 | 4,415 | 4,556 |
| 1952 | 514 | 4,969 | 5,051 |
| 1953 | 544 | 5,588 | 5,621 |
| 1954 | 561 | 5,844 | 6,580 |
| 1955 | 603 | 6,762 | 6,941 |
| 1956 | 628 | 7,242 | 7,938 |
| 1957 | 647 | 8,081 | 8,804 |
| 1958 | 665 | 7,816 | 9,793 |
| 1959 | 700 | 8,852 | 10,277 |
| 1960 | 719 | 9,717 | 10,161 |
| 1961 | 738 | 9,752 | 10,824 |
| 1962 | 767 | 10,591 | 11,623 |
| 1963 | 805 | 11,397 | 12,329 |
| 1964 | 847 | 12,216 | 12,985 |
| 1965 | 888 | 12,723 | 13,392 |
| 1966 | 932 | 12,857 | 14,391 |

# Motor Vehicle Factory Sales, U. S. Plants

| | PASSENGER CARS | | MOTOR TRUCKS AND BUSES | | TOTAL | |
|---|---|---|---|---|---|---|
| | Number | Value (000) | Number | Value (000) | Number | Value (000) |
| 1900 ....... | 4,192 | $ 4,899 | ......... | ......... | 4,192 | $ 4,899 |
| 1901 ....... | 7,000 | 8,183 | ......... | ......... | 7,000 | 8,183 |
| 1902 ....... | 9,000 | 10,395 | ......... | ......... | 9,000 | 10,395 |
| 1903 ....... | 11,235 | 13,000 | ......... | ......... | 11,235 | 13,000 |
| 1904 ....... | 22,130 | 23,358 | 700 | $ 1,273 | 22,830 | 24,630 |
| 1905 ....... | 24,250 | 38,670 | 750 | 1,330 | 25,000 | 40,000 |
| 1906 ....... | 33,200 | 61,460 | 800 | 1,440 | 34,000 | 62,900 |
| 1907 ....... | 43,000 | 91,620 | 1,000 | 1,780 | 44,000 | 93,400 |
| 1908 ....... | 63,500 | 135,250 | 1,500 | 2,550 | 65,000 | 137,800 |
| 1909 ....... | 123,990 | 159,766 | 3,297 | 5,334 | 127,287 | 165,099 |
| 1910 ....... | 181,000 | 215,340 | 6,000 | 9,660 | 187,000 | 225,000 |
| 1911 ....... | 199,319 | 225,000 | 10,681 | 21,000 | 210,000 | 246,000 |
| 1912 ....... | 356,000 | 335,000 | 22,000 | 43,000 | 378,000 | 378,000 |
| 1913 ....... | 461,500 | 399,902 | 23,500 | 44,000 | 485,000 | 443,902 |
| 1914 ....... | 548,139 | 420,838 | 24,900 | 44,219 | 573,039 | 465,057 |
| 1915 ....... | 895,930 | 575,978 | 74,000 | 125,800 | 969,930 | 701,778 |
| 1916 ....... | 1,525,578 | 921,378 | 92,130 | 161,000 | 1,617,708 | 1,082,378 |
| 1917 ....... | 1,745,792 | 1,053,506 | 128,157 | 220,983 | 1,873,949 | 1,274,488 |
| 1918 ....... | 943,436 | 801,938 | 227,250 | 434,169 | 1,170,686 | 1,236,107 |
| 1919 ....... | 1,651,625 | 1,365,395 | 224,731 | 371,423 | 1,876,356 | 1,736,818 |
| 1920 ....... | 1,905,560 | 1,809,171 | 321,789 | 423,249 | 2,227,349 | 2,232,420 |
| 1921 ....... | 1,468,067 | 1,038,191 | 148,052 | 166,071 | 1,616,119 | 1,204,262 |
| 1922 ....... | 2,274,185 | 1,494,514 | 269,991 | 226,050 | 2,544,176 | 1,720,564 |
| 1923 ....... | 3,624,717 | 2,196,272 | 409,295 | 308,538 | 4,034,012 | 2,504,810 |
| 1924 ....... | 3,185,881 | 1,970,097 | 416,659 | 318,581 | 3,602,540 | 2,288,677 |
| 1925 ....... | 3,735,171 | 2,458,370 | 530,659 | 458,400 | 4,265,830 | 2,916,770 |
| 1926 ....... | 3,692,317 | 2,607,365 | 608,617 | 484,823 | 4,300,934 | 3,092,188 |
| 1927 ....... | 2,936,533 | 2,164,671 | 464,793 | 420,131 | 3,401,326 | 2,584,802 |
| 1928 ....... | 3,775,417 | 2,572,599 | 583,342 | 460,109 | 4,358,759 | 3,032,708 |
| 1929 ....... | 4,455,178 | 2,790,614 | 881,909 | 622,534 | 5,337,087 | 3,413,148 |
| 1930 ....... | 2,787,456 | 1,644,083 | 575,364 | 390,752 | 3,362,820 | 2,034,835 |
| 1931 ....... | 1,948,164 | 1,108,247 | 432,262 | 265,445 | 2,380,426 | 1,373,691 |
| 1932 ...;... | 1,103,557 | 616,860 | 228,303 | 137,624 | 1,331,860 | 754,485 |
| 1933 ....... | 1,560,599 | 773,425 | 329,218 | 175,381 | 1,889,817 | 948,806 |
| 1934 ....... | 2,160,865 | 1,140,478 | 576,205 | 326,782 | 2,737,070 | 1,467,260 |
| 1935 ....... | 3,273,874 | 1,707,836 | 697,367 | 380,997 | 3,971,241 | 2,088,834 |
| 1936 ....... | 3,679,242 | 2,014,747 | 782,220 | 463,719 | 4,461,462 | 2,478,467 |
| 1937 ....... | 3,929,203 | 2,240,913 | 891,016 | 537,315 | 4,820,219 | 2,778,227 |
| 1938 ....... | 2,019,566 | 1,241,032 | 488,841 | 329,918 | 2,508,407 | 1,570,950 |
| 1939 ....... | 2,888,512 | 1,770,232 | 700,377 | 489,787 | 3,588,889 | 2,260,018 |

| | | | | | |
|---|---|---|---|---|---|
| 1940 ....... 3,717,385 | 2,370,654 | 754,901 | 567,820 | 4,472,286 | 2,938,474 |
| 1941 ....... 3,779,682 | 2,567,206 | 1,060,820 | 1,069,800 | 4,840,502 | 3,637,006 |
| 1942 ....... 222,862 | 163,814 | 818,662 | 1,427,457 | 1,041,524 | 1,591,270 |
| 1943 ....... 139 | 102 | 699,689 | 1,451,794 | 699,828 | 1,451,896 |
| 1944 ....... 610 | 447 | 737,524 | 1,700,929 | 738,134 | 1,701,376 |
| 1945 ....... 69,532 | 57,255 | 655,683 | 1,181,956 | 725,215 | 1,239,210 |
| 1946 ....... 2,148,699 | 1,979,781 | 940,963 | 1,043,247 | 3,089,662 | 3,023,028 |
| 1947 ....... 3,558,178 | 3,936,017 | 1,239,443 | 1,731,713 | 4,797,621 | 5,667,730 |
| 1948 ....... 3,909,270 | 4,870,423 | 1,376,274 | 1,880,475 | 5,285,544 | 6,750,898 |
| 1949 ....... 5,119,466 | 6,650,857 | 1,134,185 | 1,394,035 | 6,253,651 | 8,044,892 |
| 1950 ....... 6,665,863 | 8,468,137 | 1,337,193 | 1,707,748 | 8,003,056 | 10,175,885 |
| 1951 ....... 5,338,435 | 7,241,275 | 1,426,828 | 2,323,859 | 6,765,263 | 9,565,134 |
| 1952 ....... 4,320,794 | 6,455,114 | 1,218,165 | 2,319,789 | 5,538,959 | 8,774,903 |
| 1953 ....... 6,116,948 | 9,002,580 | 1,206,266 | 2,089,060 | 7,323,214 | 11,091,640 |
| 1954 ....... 5,558,897 | 8,218,094 | 1,042,174 | 1,660,019 | 6,601,071 | 9,878,113 |
| 1955 ....... 7,920,186 | 12,452,871 | 1,249,106 | 2,020,973 | 9,169,292 | 14,473,844 |
| 1956 ....... 5,816,109 | 9,754,971 | 1,104,481 | 2,077,432 | 6,920,590 | 11,832,403 |
| 1957 ....... 6,113,344 | 11,198,379 | 1,107,176 | 2,082,723 | 7,220,520 | 13,281,102 |
| 1958 ....... 4,257,812 | 8,010,366 | 877,294 | 1,730,027 | 5,135,106 | 9,740,393 |
| 1959 ....... 5,591,243 | 10,534,421 | 1,137,386 | 2,338,719 | 6,728,629 | 12,873,140 |
| 1960 ....... 6,674,796 | 12,164,234 | 1,194,475 | 2,350,680 | 7,869,271 | 14,514,914 |
| 1961 ....... 5,542,707 | 10,285,777 | 1,133,804 | 2,155,753 | 6,676,511 | 12,441,530 |
| 1962 ....... 6,933,240 | 13,071,709 | 1,240,168 | 2,581,756 | 8,173,408 | 15,653,465 |
| 1963 ....... 7,637,728 | 14,427,077 | 1,462,708 | 3,090,345 | 9,100,436 | 17,517,422 |
| 1964 ....... 7,751,822 | 14,836,822 | 1,540,453 | 3,223,569 | 9,292,275 | 18,060,391 |
| 1965 ....... 9,305,561 | 18,380,036 | 1,751,805 | 3,733,664 | 11,057,366 | 22,113,700 |
| 1966* ...... 8,598,326 | 17,600,000 | 1,731,084 | 3,900,000 | 10,329,410 | 21,500,000 |

NOTE: A substantial proportion of the trucks and buses consists of chassis only; therefore the value of the bodies for these chassis is not included. Value is based on vehicles with standard equipment. Prior to July 1, 1964 certain firms included tactical vehicles in factory sales data. After July 1, 1964 all tactical vehicles are excluded. Federal excise taxes are excluded.           *Preliminary.

SOURCE: Automobile Manufacturers Association.

**46% OF CAR TRIPS RELATED TO EARNING A LIVING**

45.8%
EARNING A LIVING
(To and From Work
Business Calls)

7.6%
EDUCATIONAL, CIVIC
AND RELIGIOUS

29.5%
FAMILY BUSINESS
(Shopping, Medical
and Dental, Etc.)

17.1%
SOCIAL & RECREATIONAL
(Pleasure Rides,
Vacations, Etc.)

PERCENT OF TRIPS

SOURCE: U. S. DEPARTMENT OF COMMERCE, BUREAU OF PUBLIC ROADS

# Automobiles Owned by 79 Percent of U. S. Families

| Year | Number Families (Millions) | Percent Owning Automobiles | Number Owning Automobiles (Millions) |
|---|---|---|---|
| 1941 | — | 51 | — |
| 1948 | 42.5 | 54 | 23 |
| 1949 | 44.1 | 56 | 25 |
| 1950 | 45.7 | 60 | 27 |
| 1951 | 46.3 | 65 | 30 |
| 1952 | 47.2 | 65 | 31 |
| 1953 | 48.0 | 65 | 31 |
| 1954 | 48.7 | 70 | 34 |
| 1955 | 49.3 | 71 | 35 |
| 1956 | 50.4 | 73 | 36 |
| 1957 | 51.2 | 75 | 39 |
| 1958 | 52.0 | 73 | 38 |
| 1959 | 52.5 | 74 | 39 |
| 1960 | 53.4 | 77 | 41 |
| 1961 | 54.2 | 76 | 41 |
| 1962 | 54.9 | 74 | 41 |
| 1963 | 56.5 | 80 | 45 |
| 1964 | 56.8 | 78 | 44 |
| 1965 | 58.4 | 79 | 46 |
| 1966 | 59.1 | 79 | 47 |

SOURCE: "Survey of Consumer Finances," Federal Reserve Board; and Survey Research Center, University of Michigan.

# One U.S. Business in Six is Automotive

| | Number of Establishments | Number of Employees | Sales (Thousands) |
|---|---|---|---|
| **retail** | | | |
| Motor Vehicle Dealers, Franchised, Non-Franchised: Tire, Battery, Accessory Dealers . . . . | 87,232 | 834,815 | $ 43,797,494 |
| Gasoline Service Stations . . . . . . . . . . . . . . . . . . . | 211,473 | 732,542 | 17,759,917 |
| Total Retail . . . . . . . . . . . . . . . . . . . . . . . . . | 298,705 | 1,567,357 | $ 61,557,411 |
| Percent of All Retail Business . . . . . . . . . . . . . | 17.5% | 15.7% | 25.2% |

255

# wholesale

| | | | |
|---|---|---|---|
| Motor Vehicles, Automotive Equipment . . . . . . . . . | 28,895 | 307,732 | $ 36,583,709 |
| Petroleum Bulk Stations, Terminals . . . . . . . . . . . . | 30,873 | 151,613 | 21,485,414 |
| Total Wholesale . . . . . . . . . . . . . . . . . . . . . . . | 59,768 | 459,345 | $ 58,069,123 |
| Percent of All Wholesale Business . . . . . . . . . . | 19.3% | 14.2% | 16.2% |

# service

| | | | |
|---|---|---|---|
| Auto Repair Services, Garages . . . . . . . . . . . . . . . | 139,611 | 425,340 | $ 5,443,938 |
| Motels, Tourist Courts, Trailer Parks . . . . . . . . . . . | 55,170 | 242,821 | 2,153,201 |
| Total Service. . . . . . . . . . . . . . . . . . . . . . . . . . | 194,781 | 668,161 | $ 7,597,139 |
| Percent of All Service Business . . . . . . . . . . . . . | 18.3% | 15.3% | 17.0% |
| GRAND TOTAL . . . . . . . . . . . . . . . . . . . . . . | 553,254 | 2,694,863 | $127,223,673 |
| Percent of All U.S. Retail, Wholesale and Service Sales. . . . . . . . . . . . . . . . . . . . . . | 18.0% | 15.3% | 19.7% |

SOURCE: U.S. Department of Commerce, Bureau of the Census, 1963 Census of Business.

# index

## a

A.A.A., see American Automobile Association
A.B.C. thread standard, 118
A.C.F. Motors, 81
accessory equipment, 70, 81; see also specific accessories: heaters, radios, etc.
Adams-Farwell, 39
advertising, 22, 56, 61, 83, 85, 114
air cleaners, 75, 85, 144
air conditioning, 104, 132, 154
Allison, James A., 33
Allstate automobile, 127
aluminum, use in automobiles, 20, 62, 140; see also individual entries: bodies, fenders, etc.
ambulances, 23
American Austin Car Co., 89
American Automobile Association, 27, 131, 138
American Bantam Co., 138
American La France Fire Engine Co., 51
American Motor Car Manufacturers Assoc., 37
American Motor League, 14
American Motors Corp., 132, 134, 152, 154
Anderson, John W., 31
antifreeze solutions, 152
Apperson, Edgar, 12, 179
Apperson, Elmer, 179
Argonaut Motor Machine Corp., 145
Ariel automobile, 37
Association of Licensed Automobile Manufacturers, 31, 42, 53
atomic bomb test using motor vehicles, 130
Austin Bantam automobile, 90
Auto Wagon automobile, 42
Autocar Co., 21, 43, 69, 129

"Automobile" (use of term for motor vehicles), 17
Automobile Blue Book, 25
Automobile Board of Trade, 53, 54, 55
Automobile Club of America, 20, 22, 25, 29
Automobile Club of Great Britain and Ireland Reliability Trial, 32
Automobile Daily News, 82
Automobile Information Disclosure Act, 147
Automobile Manufacturers Assoc., 96, 97, 112, 129, 132, 134, 138, 140, 143, 146, 150, 152
Automobile Topics, 23
Automobile Committee for Air Defense, 106
Automotive Council for War Production, 108, 109, 110
Automotive Golden Jubilee, 115
Automotive News, 82
Automotive Safety Foundation, 141
Automotive Service Industries Assoc., 148
axles, 89

## b

back-up lights, 75
Baker, E. G. ("Cannon Ball"), 78, 83
Barnum & Bailey Circus, 16
Barthel, Oliver E., 16†
batteries, 38, 96, 101
Beck, C. D. and Co., Inc., 139
beds, convertible, 57, 98
Bendix, Vincent, 180
Bennett, Charles H., 31
Benz, Karl, 6
Besserdich, William, 46
Bezner, Frederick O., 39
bodies, 26, 27, 69
    aluminum, 38, 59, 62, 88

†Illustration

257

four-door, 52, 76, 98
steel, 55, 77, 96
seating arrangements, 58, 59
double-cowl, 61
enclosed, 73, 75, 77, 81, 89
streamlining designs, 85, 94
closed bodies comprise 90% of cars sold, 89
Fisher Body's "No-Draft Ventilation," 94
doors made wider, 96
sloping side windows appear, 99
unitized, 104, 145
see also specific types: tonneau, coupe, sedan, etc.
body finishes, see paints and finishes
Borg-Warner Corp., 122
Brady, James J., 40
brakes, 40, 41
air, 35
hand brake, 58, 98
hydraulic, 67, 86
four-wheel, 67, 70, 80, 85
vacuum, 85, 86
power, 89, 94
emergency braking systems, 99
self-adjusting, 116, 151, 154
bonded, 120
suspended brake pedal offered, 128
aluminum drums, 144
flanged drum introduced, 147
automatic release of parking brake, 151
Brayton, George B., 13
Breer, Carl, 24, 73, 85
Breer Engineering Co., 77
brick-surfaced roads, 12
Briggs Mfg. Co., 131
Briscoe automobile, 61†
Briscoe, Benjamin, 28, 50, 180
Briscoe, Frank, 28, 180
Brockaway, George, 55
Brockaway Motor Co., 55, 87, 139
Brockway truck, 54†
Brownlow-Latimer Federal Good Roads Bill, 33
Brush, Alanson P., 41
Budd, Edward G., 55
Buick automobile
6-cylinder engine adopted, 59
8-cylinder engine adopted, 92
3,000,000th built, 99
model changeover made in 10 days, 41
Dynaflow hydraulic torque converter introduced, 118
hardtop convertible, 120†
XP 300 experimental car, 125
V-8 engine offered, 125
Century series, 133†
Special, 152
Buick Autovim & Power Co., 26
Buick, David D., 26, 180
Buick Motor Co., 31, 45
bumpers, 39, 69, 82
buses, 38, 87, 154; see also specific makes: White, Reo, etc.

**C**

Cadillac automobile
first car completed, 28
Dewar Trophy, 44, 56
electric starter, 54, 56
V-8 engine, 58
syncro-mesh transmission, 86
V-12 engine, 89
V-16 engine, 89
power brakes, 89
Cadillac Automobile Co., 28, 33
Cadillac Division of General Motors Corp., 48
Cadillac Motor Car Co., 28, 48, 74
"California Top," 33
carburetors, 7, 11, 24
twin, 41
thermostatic control, 73
down-draft, 88
intake silencers, 89
Chalmers, Hugh, 181
Chandler automobile, 86
Chapin, Roy D., 26, 39, 181
chassis
"simplified," 53
Studebaker gold chassis, 62
rubber chassis springs by Graham-Paige, 89
Chevrolet chassis without X-member, 98
Checker Motors Corp., 147
Checker Superba, 61, 147
Chevrolet automobile
first car, 47
4-cylinder engine, 58
V-8 engine, 64
6-cylinder engine replaces 4-cylinder, 87
production highlights, 96, 102, 124
steel station wagon, 97†
vacuum operated gearshift, 102
Impala series, 146†
Chevrolet Div. of G.M., 67, 116, 130, 138
Chevrolet, Louis, 47, 182
Chevrolet Motor Co. of Mich., 53, 56, 67

†Illustration

Chevrolet truck, 138, 143, 148
Chicago Times-Herald Race, 13
chokes, automatic, 93
chromium plating, 81
Chrysler automobile, 77, 93, 96, 119†, 120, 121, 122, 210†
Chrysler Corp.
   formed, 82
   pays $10,000,000 in dividends, 86
   purchases Dodge Bros., 87
   Plymouth, De Soto introduced, 87
   8-cylinder engine, 89
   "Superfinish" method, 102
   San Leandro plant opened, 118
   Silver anniversary, 124
   Detroit Tank Arsenal transferred to Chrysler, 128
   proving grounds at Chelsea, 129, 134
   purchases Briggs auto plants, 131
   loan obtained from Prudential Insurance, 132
   buys Universal Products Co., 135
   Twinsburg, Ohio plant, 136
   25 millionth vehicle produced, 144
   purchases stock in Simca, 145
   car divisions realigned, 148
   dedicates St. Louis plant, 152
Chrysler, Walter, 67, 77, 182
cigar lighters, 81
circuses, use of motor vehicles, 16, 65
Clarke, Louis S., 19, 28
Cleveland Vehicle Co., 59
Clifton, Charles, 65, 182
clutches
   centrifugal, 35
   multiple disc, 53
   vacuum-operated, 93
   automatic clutch with semi-automatic transmission, 106
   suspended clutch pedal offered, 128
Coffin, Howard E., 39
colors, see paints and finishes
Columbia Electric truck, 32
Comet, 151, 210†
Commercial Car Manufacturers Assoc., 46
concrete mixers, truck, 86
concrete pavement, first mile of, 47
Continental automobile, 135†
Continental Motors Corp., 126
convertible bodies, 33, 59, 70, 92, 102†
cooling systems, 28, 37; see also radiators
Cord automobile, 90†, 100†
Corvair, 151
Corvette, 131
Cosmopolitan Race, 16

Couzens, James, 30
Crocker, Sewall K., 30†
Crosley automobile, 103†, 115†, 123, 128
Crosley Corp., 112, 122, 123, 128
Crosley, Powell, Jr., 103†
cross licensing, see patent licensing agreements
Cugnot, Nicolas, 5
Curtiss-Wright Corp., 150
cyclecars, 58
cylinder casting, 48

# d

Daimler, Gottlieb, 6
DaVinci, Leonardo, 5
dashboards, see instrument panels
Day, George H., 31
dealers and dealerships, 20, 21
Dearborn Motors Corp., 129
defrosters, 99
De Sakhnoffsky, (Count) Alexis, 98
design, see bodies
De Soto automobile, 155
   introduced, 87
   vacuum-operated clutch, 93
   "Airflow," 95
   automatic transmission overdrive, 96
   nine-passenger station wagon, 121
   V-8 engine offered, 128
Detroit, early auto industry, 25, 40
Detroit Tank Arsenal, 128
Dewar Trophy, 45, 56
Diamond T Motor Car Co., 38, 53, 145
Dietz, R. E., Co., 23
directional signals, 102
disabled veterans' cars, 115
Divco Truck Division, 139
Dodge automobile, 58, 77, 120, 121, 130†, 149–51
Dodge Bros. Inc., 87
Dodge, Horace, 29, 58, 183
Dodge, John, 29, 58, 183
Dodge trucks, 123
Dort automobile, 71†
Drake, J. Walter, 74
"drive-it-yourself," see rentals and leasing
driver education and training, 117, 127
drivers licenses, 21, 23
Dual Motors Corp., 136, 138
dual-control cars, 118
Duesenberg automobile, 70, 91†
Duesenberg, Frederick S., 184
du Pont, Pierre S., 70

†*Illustration*

Durant automobile, 77†
Durant Motors Inc., 76
Durant, William C., 43, 70, 76, 77†, 184
Duryea automobile, 10†, 15, 17
Duryea, Charles E., 10†, 13, 185
Duryea, J. Frank, 10†, 15†
Duryea Motor Wagon Co., 13, 15
Dyke, A. L., 21

**e**

Eaton, William, 43
economy runs and contests, 42, 62
Edgar, Graham, 84
electric automobiles, 16, 23, 53, 78, 148
Electric Vehicle Co., 26, 29
electrical systems, 128, 132, 152
electrochemical fuel conversion, 148
Ellerbeck, B. B., 92
Elliott, Sterling, 29
engine mountings, rubber 72, 82, 92, 93
engines
    air-cooled, 20, 37, 40†, 150
    moved under hood, 23, 29
    valve-in-head, 20, 32
    six-cylinder, 39, 40, 79, 132
    rotary, 39, 150
    twelve-cylinder, 39, 61, 89, 94, 149
    eight-cylinder, 42, 58, 70, 80, 88, 89, 132
    sleeve-valve, 46, 51, 73†
    V-8, 42, 58, 62, 93†, 118, 126†, 128, 132, 135, 137, 152
    L-head, 77
    V-16, 89
    superchargers, 94
    interchangeable 6- or 8-cylinder engines on a basic frame, 106
    high-compression, for high-octane fuel, 118
    gas turbine, 126, 133, 140, 143, 148
    free-piston type, 139
    V-4, 140
    aluminum, 150, 152
    nuclear-powered, 148
Erskine, Albert R., 186
Erskine automobile, 84
Essex automobile, 68†
Essex Motor Car Co., 64
Ethyl Corp., 77
Evans, Oliver, 5
exhaust vapors, elimination of, 151
experimental cars, 15†, 125, 129, 133, 137, 145, 146, 148, 152

**f**

factories, concrete reinforced, 31
Fageol Motors Co., 81, 85
Falcon, 151
Federal Aid Road Act, 63
fenders
    aluminum, 62
    full-skirted, 93
    covers for rear fenders, 94, 96
    extended to middle of front door, 106
Ferguson, Harry, Inc., 129
filters, gasoline and oil, 80, 85
financing, see installment buying
fire-fighting apparatus, 51
firsts in connection with automobile, see subject entries: magazines, purchases, roads, etc.
Fischer automobile, 35
Fisher Body Co., 46, 69, 82, 84
Fisher, Carl G., 33, 48, 57
Fisher, Charles T., 46, 186
Fisher, Frederic J., 46, 186
"flat-rate" repair system, 68
*Fleet Owner*, 87
Fleetwood Body Corp., 82
Flint automobile, 79†
flying automobiles, 100, 110, 147
Ford automobile, 224†
    "Quadricycle," 15†
    "999," 30†, 32
    model "T," 43, 55, 79, 85, 144
    model "A," 84†, 93
    V-8, 93†, 118, 142†
    Thunderbird, 145†, 247†
Ford, Edsel B., 69
Ford, Henry, 15†, 29, 69, 187
Ford, Henry, II, 112†
Ford Motor Co.
    incorporated, 29
    opens first branch, 35
    Selden Patent Case, 32, 47, 52
    Highland Park plant, 42, 51
    production highlights, 56, 58, 68, 72, 77, 78, 80, 106, 144
    $5.00 daily wage, 58
    rebate plan, 58, 61
    Rouge plant, 63
    financial crisis of 1921, 72
    buys Lincoln Motor Co., 76
    prices reduced by $50.00, 76
    weekly purchase plan, 77
    manufacturers accessories for Ford cars, 80
    5-day work week, 84

†*Illustration*

$7.00 daily wage, 88
participates in National Auto Show, 97
spends $40 million for plant expansion, 102
exhibits at 1941 National Auto Show, 106
resumes production of autos after WW II, 112†
Los Angeles assembly plant opened, 118
Ford Div. organized, 120
Mahwah, N. J. factory, 130, 135
proving grounds at Romeo, 134
Nashville glass plant, 135
stock offered to public, 138
purchases Sherman Products, 152
Ford Motor Credit Co., 149
Fordson tractor, 63
foreign activities of U.S. auto firms, 74
four-wheel drive, 46, 50, 57
Four Wheel Drive Auto Co., 50, 145
frame construction, pressed steel, 31
Franklin automobile, 40†
Frazer, E. M., 85
Frazer, Joseph W., 110
free-wheeling, 89, 92, 93
Fry, Vernon, 31
fuel economy, 94
fuel injection, 140
Furber, Frederick, 65

**g**

garages, see service stations
gas turbines, see engines
gasoline
    ethyl, 74, 77, 80
    octane scale devised, 84
    high-octane, 118
gasoline-electric automobiles, 45
gasoline gauges, 76
gasoline stations, see service stations
gears, 42, 43, 57, 85
gearshifts
    "H" slot, 29
    located on dashboard, 97, 107, 134
    finger-tip control, on steering column, 97, 101
    automatic gearshift, 101
    gearshift control on steering column, 101
    vacuum-operated, 102
General Motors Acceptance Corp., 69
General Motors Co., 43

General Motors Corp.
    acquires Buick, Oldsmobile, Oakland & Rapid Motor Vehicle Co., 46
    Cadillac becomes part of GM, 48
    stock dividend payments, 48, 60, 85
    Chevrolet becomes part of GM, 69
    buys interest in Fisher Body Co., 69
    GM building, 74
    proving grounds, 80, 125, 129
    acquires Yellow Truck & Coach Co., 81
    buys Fisher Body Corp., 84
    offers all-steel turret tops, 96
    Wilmington, Del. plant opened, 118
    Framingham, Mass. plant opened, 118
    "Transportation Unlimited" show, 120
    purchases Euclid Road Machinery stock, 130
    transmission plant fire, 131
    production highlights, 134
General Motors Research Corp., 70
General Motors truck, 24, 62
General Motors Truck Co., 53
General Tire and Rubber Co., 132
generators, 96, 150
glass, safety, 82
Glidden, Charles J., 35, 187
Glidden tours, 35, 37†, 45, 48
governors, 24
Grabowsky, Max, 28
Graham, Roy A., 188
Graham-Paige Motors Corp., 85, 109, 110, 117
Gramm, B. A., 32
Gray, John S., 31
guarantees, see warranties

**h**

Hall, E. J., 64
Hammond, E. T., 31
Harroun, Ray, 53
Haynes automobile, 12, 13†, 20
Haynes, Elwood G., 12, 13†, 76, 188
Haynes-Apperson automobile, 20
headlamps, 33, 83
    kerosene, 23
    acetylene, 33
    electric-acetylene, 49
    tilt-beam, 60
    prism lenses, 61
    dimmer switches, 77, 128
    two-filament bulbs, 80
    sealed-beam, 104, 134, 138

†*Illustration*

concealed in front fenders, 107
dual-headlighting system, 138, 140, 150
  automatically turned on, 151
heating and ventilation, 65, 70, 84, 101,
  104; *see also* air conditioning, 134
Herrington, Arthur W., 93, 104
Hewitt Motor Car Co., 42, 53
Highway Act of 1956, 139
Highway Research Board, 72
highways, see roads
hill climbs, 20, 43
Hines, Edward N., 53
Holcomb, Bert, 19†
hoods, lock releases, 103
horns, 38, 46
horse power rating formula, 42
*Horseless Age*, 14
Howie, Robert G., 104
Hudson automobile, 46†, 53, 80, 97, 99,
  143
Hudson Motor Car Co., 32, 48
Hupmobile automobile, 68†, 69†, 92, 95,
  97
Hupmobile Motor Car Corp., 88, 121

# i

ignition systems, 11, 48, 121, 124, 151
Imperial automobile, 149†
Indiana Truck Corp., 87, 94
Indianapolis 500-Mile Race, 53
Indianapolis Speedway, 48
installment buying, 37, 56, 77, 106, 121,
  124, 126
instrument panels, 69, 134, 151
insurance, 19, 74
International Harvester Co., 41, 102, 153
International motor truck, 42†, 128

# j

Jackson, H. Nelson, 30†
"Jeep," 104; *see also* Willys-Overland
  vehicles
Jeffery automobile, 57
Jeffery, Thomas B., 24, 189
Jeffery, Thomas B., Co., 28, 62
jitneys, 60
Jordan, Edward 84, 189
Jordan Motor Co., 84
Joy, Henry B., 190

# k

Kaiser automobile, 116†
Kaiser, Henry, 110
Kaiser Industries Corp., 136
Kaiser Motors Corp., 134, 136
Kaiser-Frazer Corp., 113, 114, 118, 129
Keeshin Transcontinental Run, 98
Kelly-Springfield Co., 65
Kelvinator Corporation, 99
kerosene, used as fuel, 66
Kettering, Charles F., 54, 70, 118, 190
King automobile, 16†
King, Charles B., 14, 16†, 28, 191
Kissel automobile, 56, 70†, 71†
Knight, Charles Y., 46
Knight sleeve-valve engine, see engines,
  sleeve-valve
Knudsen, William S., 104, 191
Kurtis-Kraft, Inc., 121

# l

labor strikes, 113
Lafayette Motors Corp., 80
Lancer, 152
Lanchester Vibration dampener, 70
Lark, 147, 150, 160, 164
latches, trunk and door, 137, 138, 141,
  147, 151
laws and legislation, 18, 26, 28, 33, 38,
  42, 55, 63, 67, 109, 139, 147; *see
  also specific legislation:* Red Flag
  Law, Federal Aid Road Act., etc.
leasing, see rentals and leasing
Lee, Gordon, 74
Leland and Faulconer Mfg. Co., 33
Leland, Henry M., 64, 192
Le Vassor, Emile, 6
Liberty aircraft engines, 64
Liberty Bell, at Panama-Pacific Exposition,
  60
Lincoln automobile, 96† (Lincoln-Zephyr)
Lincoln Highway, 57
Lincoln Motor Co., 64, 74
Lincoln-Mercury Division of Ford, 129, 151
Little Motor Car Co., 56
locks, see latches
Locomobile automobile, 29
Loomis, Gilbert, 19
Lougheed, Malcolm, 67, 70, 86
lubrication, 33, 56, 84, 135, 154

†*Illustration*

## m

Macauley, Alvan, 192
Mack Bros. Motor Car Co., 22, 53, 85, 124
Mack bus, 22, 143
Mack truck, 52†
Mack Truck, Inc., 139, 143
Mackinac Bridge, 143
magazines, 14
magnetos, 26, 48
Major Award Trophy, 80
Malcolmson, Alex Y., 29
manifolds, 64, 89, 98
Marmon automobile and racing car, 53, 62
Marmon, Howard C., 193
Marmon-Herrington Co., Inc., 123
Marmon, Walter C., 93
Marquette automobile, 87†
Marriott, Fred, 38, 39†
Mason, George W., 100, 193
Matheson, Charles W., 194
Matter, Louis, 134
Maxim, Hiram P., 13, 16, 19†
Maxwell Motor Co., 72
Maxwell automobile, 41†
Maxwell, Jonathan D., 12, 28, 194
Maxwell-Chalmers Corp., 79, 82
Mayback, Wilhelm, 6
mechanics, see service men
Mercury, 101
Mercury-Edsel-Lincoln Div. of Ford, 145
Metz, Charles, 195
Metzger, William E., 20
Michigan State College, 128
Midgley, Thomas, Jr., 75
mirrors, 53, 81, 85, 144, 147, 151
Mobile Steamer, 23†
model announcement dates, 91, 96, 97, 98, 122
Montpelier Mfg. Co., 122
Morgan, William, 19
Morill, George H., 15
Morris and Salom Electrobat, 17
Motorcycle, 14
Motor, 31, 80
Motor Age, 21
Mueller, Oscar, 14
Mueller-Benz automobile, 14
mufflers, 154
Murdock, J. M., 45†
Murphy, Edward M., 41

## n

NSU Werke, 150

Narraganset Park race, 16†, 17
Nash automobile, 64†, 88, 98, 104, 107†, 122, 143
Nash, Charles W., 62, 99, 195
Nash Motors Co.
  formed, 62
  truck production for U.S. Army, 67
  buys interest in Seaman Body, 69
  buys Lafayette Motors Corp., 80
  stock held by employees, 85
  merges with Kelvinator, 99
Nash-Kelvinator Corp., 99, 122, 123, 132
National Association of Automobile Advertising Men, 56
National Association of Automobile Manufacturers, 24, 56
National Association of Retail Automobile Dealers, 35
National Automobile Chamber of Commerce, 56, 59, 63, 74, 89, 91, 96
National Automobile Dealers Assoc., 67
New York and Ohio Co., 21
New York Stock Exchange, lists securities of auto companies, 53
New York-to-Buffalo endurance run, 24
New York-to-Paris Race, 44
New York-to-Portland Race, 37
New York-to-St. Louis tour, 34†, 35
nickel plate trim, 42
Nic-l-Silver Battery Co., 148
Nixon, Richard M., 140
Northern automobile, 28

## o

Oakland Motor Car Co., 41, 45, 91
Ohio Automobile Co., 28
"Old Pacific," 31
Oldfield, Berner Eli ("Barney"), 30†, 32
Olds Motor Works, 20, 28, 33
Olds, Ransom E., 18, 20, 33, 196
Olds Motor Vehicle Co., 19
Oldsmobile automobile, 18, 19, 27†, 36†, 76, 92, 93, 105†, 120, 121, 126†
Oldsmobile Division of G.M., 45
Oldsmobile F-85, 152
Oliver Corp., 152
ordinances, see laws and legislation
Otto, Nikolaus August, 5
Overland automobile, 32†
Overland Automobile Co., 46
Owen automobile, 49†
Owen, Percy, 21

†Illustration

263

# p

Packard automobile, 21, 59, 61, 73, 92†, 136†, 140, 145
Packard, James W., 21, 196
Packard Motor Car Co.
  patents a gearshift "H" slot, 29
  moves to Detroit, 31
  straight "8" engine introduced, 77
  hypoid gears offered, 86
  millionth car produced, 117
  merges with Studebaker, 132
Packard, Warren D., 21
Paige, Fred O., 196, 197
Paige-Detroit Motor Car Co., 85
paints and finishes
  baked enamel, 46
  pyroxolin, 81
  color ranges and variations, 103
  finishes requiring less wax, 147
parades, 55
parts, manufacturing methods, 102, 128
parts supply business, 21
patent licensing agreements, 63
Peerless automobile, 31, 75
Pennington automobile, 12
Pennington, Edward J., 12
phaeton bodies, 76
Philadelphia Commercial Wagon Parade, 55
Phillips, (Mrs.) John, H., 21
Pierce, George M., 25
Pierce, Percy, 37
Pierce-Arrow automobile, 25, 37, 45, 53, 93
Pierce-Arrow Motor Car Co., 87, 183
Pierce-Arrow truck, 53
"piggy-back" R.R. service, see trucks
Pikes Peak, 23
pistons, 59, 89, 107
Pittsburgh Motor Vehicle Co., 19, 21
Plymouth automobile
  introduced, 87
  "floating power" offered, 92
  vacuum-powered convertible top, 102
  4 millionth car built, 106
  steel station wagon, 121
  10 millionth car built, 141
  gas turbine model, 133
  1957 models, 142
Pontiac automobile, 89, 91, 101, 140, 152
  introduced, 83
  production highlights, 98, 147
  begins taxicab line, 104
  Tempest, 152
Pope, Albert A., 197

Pope-Columbia automobile, 19
Pope-Hartford automobile, 35
Pope-Hartford truck, 54
Pope Mfg. Co., 13, 16, 19
Post, Augustus, 35, 197
postal stamps, commemorative issues, 128, 153
power take-off, 32
President of the U.S., 23, 74, 98, 154
President's Action Committee for Highway Safety, 134
press previews, 18
Prest-O-Lite Co., 33
prices and pricing, 147
production highlights
  25 millionth vehicle produced, 82
  50 millionth vehicle produced, 92
  75 millionth vehicle produced, 102
  100 millionth vehicle produced, 118
  100 millionth passenger car produced, 127
Prudential Insurance Co. of America, 132
purchase of first car, 16

# r

races and racing, 13, 15, 17, 34, 138; see *also individual races;* Chicago Times-Herald Race, Indianapolis 500, etc.
Rackham, Horace H., 31
radiators
  cellular replaces tubular, 48
  shutters, 63
  locking caps, 81
  grills made of pressed steel, 92
  grills become V-shaped, 94
  see *also* cooling systems
Radio Corp. of America, 131
radios, 77, 88, 96, 104, 144
railway box cars, dimensions, 59
Rambler (Nash, American Motors Corp.) automobile, 123
Rambler (T. J. Jeffery Co.) automobile, 28, 58
Ramsey, (Mrs.) John R., 46
Rapid Motor Vehicle Co., 46, 53
Rapid Vehicle Co., 28
rationing, automobiles and gasoline, 109, 110
record players, offered as accessory, 138
"Red Flag" law, 18
Reo automobile, 84, 86, 95, 97, 99
Reo bus, 80
Reo Motor Car Co., 33, 99, 123
Reo Motors, Inc., 143

†*Illustration*

Reo truck, 50,
restrictions on use during war, 66, 109,
    110
Rickenbacker automobile, 77, 80, 82
Riker Electric automobile, 17
road maps, 57
Road signs, 25
roads, 12, 33
    center lines painted on, 53
    road-building codes, 58
    federal aid in construction, 63, 67, 72,
        115, 139, 145
    research on construction and mainte-
        nance, 72, 136, 137
    uniform highway numbering, 82
    Interstate Highway System, 139, 140,
        145, 153
    see also Lincoln Highway, turnpikes
roadster-coupe bodies, 75
running boards, enclosed, 104
rust prevention, 144

S

salesrooms, 21
safety
    instruction courses by Detroit police, 69
    electronic steering and braking, 131
    President's Action Committee, 134
    safety-type door latches, 137
    radar warning devices, 148
    GM's "electric fence," 152
    AMA grants for safety promotion, 152
Sampson truck, 54
San Francisco earthquake, 38
Saurer Motor Co., 53
Saxon automobile, 60
Schacht, G. A., 69
Schacht truck, 51, 69
schools for auto mechanics, 33
Schwab, Charles M., 76
Scott, John, medal, 76
scrappage of antiquated cars, 89
Seaman, Body Corp., 47, 69
Seaman, W. S. & Co., 47
Sears, Roebuck and Co., 127
seat belts, 123, 154
seats
    adjustable, 58, 101
    movable, 59
    rumble, 64, 81, 86
    safety padding offered, 101
    "Airfoam" cushions introduced, 103
    hydraulically operated, 115
    swivel front seat, 147

seat lock offered, 147
sedan bodies, hardtop models, 120, 122
Selden Patent, 13, 26; see also Ford Motor
    Co.
Selden, George B., 14, 197
Selden Patent license plates, 31
service men, 146
service stations, 21, 27, 51
Sherman Products, 152
shock absorbers, 32
shows, Detroit, 150, 153, 154
shows, New York, 22, 97, 140
side lamps, 49
Sintz, Clark, 13
Skelton, Owen R., 73, 77
Slick Airways, Inc., 136
Sloan, Alfred P., Jr., 63, 78
snow removal equipment, 76
"sociable" body, 59
Society of Automobile Engineers, 37, 50,
    59, 63, 64
Society of Automotive Engineers, 64, 81
Somewhere West of Laramie, 84
Souther, Henry, 50
spark plugs, 28
Spaulding automobile, 57
speed records, 38
speedometers, 26, 102, 141
springs and suspension
    independent front wheel suspension, 92
    "Duflex" rear springs, 101
    coil springs in rear, 101
    all-coil suspension and knee-action of-
        fered, 104
    ball joint front wheel suspension, 128
    air suspension systems, 131, 141
    torsion bar, 140, 151
standardization of parts, 49, 80, 118
Stanley Brothers, 20, 21
Stanley, F. E. and F. O., 18, 20, 198
Stanley Steamer automobile, 18, 20, 23,
    38, 39
Star automobile, 77
starting devices, 48, 52
    air, 47, 52, 54
    electric, 52, 54
    mechanical, 54
    exhaust gas, 54
    acetylene, 54
    accelerator pedal used to start engine,
        94
    ignition key, starting by, 121
station wagons, 77, 97, 105, 116, 118,
    121, 124, 125, 137, 143, 150, 151,
    154
steam cars, 20, 78
†Illustration

265

steel, 45, 48, 72, 152
steering
  Elliott principle, 29
  power, 32, 126
  left hand, 46
  "radical safety control," 99
  electronic, 131
  automatically-controlled, 146
steering wheels, 26, 151, 154
Sterling Motor Truck Co., 126, 130
Stevens, J., Arms Tool Co., 28
Stevens-Duryea automobile, 28
Stewart Motor Corp., 54
Stinson Aircraft Tooling Engr. Corp., 148
Stout, William B., 110
streamlining, see bodies, streamlining
  designs
Strelow, Albert, 29
Studebaker automobile, 33, 62, 114†,
Studebaker Bros., 19, 33
Studebaker Corp.
  formed, 53
  acquires control of Pierce-Arrow, 87
  emerges from receivership, 96
  spends $3½ million tooling for "Champion," 101
  South Bend plant purchased, 116
  merges with Packard, 132
Studebaker, John M. 198
Studebaker-Packard Corp., 132, 137, 140,
  144, 145, 147, 152, 155
student drivers, see driver education and
  training
Sturtevant automobile, 35
Stutz automobile, 74, 82
Stutz, Harry C., 198
Stutz Motor Car Co., 76, 198
sun visors, 82, 117
Superba, 147

† 

tail lamps and lights, 49
tappet adjusters, hydraulic, 90
taxes, 42, 65, 98, 126, 139, 150
taxicabs, electric, 20
telephones, installed in automobiles, 115
temperature indicators, 55, 81
theaters, drive-in, 94
Thomas, Edwin R., 39, 199
Thomas Flyer automobile, 44
Thomas taxi cab, 44
Thomas-Detroit, E. R., Co., 40
timing chains, 46
timing gears, 43

tire chains, 38
tire inflation tanks, 38
tire jacks, 81
tire rims
  demountable, 33, 60
  Goodyear Universal, 38
  clincher types, 60, 189
tires
  detachable, 26
  spare, 59, 82
  balloon type, 75, 78, 80, 83, 85
  tubeless, 118, 123, 133
  puncture-sealing, 123
  captive air-safety tire, 146
toll roads, see turnpikes
tonneau, 26
tops
  folding, 37
  "one man," 48
  offered as standard equipment, 49, 60
  all-steel turret top offered by G.M., 96
  convertible tops, vacuum-operated, 102
  plexiglass, 132
  convertible metal top, retractable, 141,
    142
torpedo body, 49
traffic signs and signals, 57, 58, 69, 76
trailers, house, 88, 99
transmissions
  sliding gear, 32, 42
  automatic, 35, 95, 101, 104, 106
  selective, 40, 48
  overdrive, 48, 96, 101, 104
  "two-range," 69
  electric drive, 45, 85
  synchro-mesh, 86, 92
  four-speed, 86
  fluid couplings for transmissions, 102
  "Hydra-Matic," 104, 106, 118, 122, 132
  "Fluid Drive," 106
  semi-automatic, with automatic clutch,
    107
  "Dynaflow," 118
  "Powerglide," 122
  "Fordomatic," 124
  "Merc-O-Matic," 124
  selector lever placed on dash, 96, 134
  push-button selector, 138, 144
  "Turboglide," 141
Tri-Car, Inc., 136
trips (by individuals)
  Cleveland to New York, 1899 (Winton),
    20
  Detroit to New York, 1901 (Chapin), 26
  San Francisco to New York, 1903 (Jackson), 30, 31

†Illustration

San Francisco to New York, 1903 (Fetch), 31
San Francisco to New York, 1903 (Whitman), 31
New York to San Francisco, 1906 (Whitman), 39
New York to Chicago, 1907 (Franklin automobile), 42
Los Angeles to New York, 1908 (Murdock), 44, 46
New York to San Francisco, 1909 (Mrs. Ramsey), 46
Denver to Los Angeles to New York by Saurer truck, 1911, 51
New York to San Francisco by Packard truck, 1912, 54
Seattle to New York by GM truck, 1916, 62
New York to Los Angeles with transmission gears locked, 1923 (Baker), 78
New York to San Francisco by GM Truck, 1926 (Baker), 83
Anchorage to Mexico City, non-stop, 1954 (Matter), 134
trucks, 38
shows, 41, 52
dump trucks, 54
tilt cab, 54, 122
WWI production, 60, 64, 67
expanded use during 1920 RR strike, 72
diesel-powered, 88, 128, 149
refrigerated, 91
Keeshin Transcontinental Run, 98
"cab-over-engine," 102
50th anniversary of trucking industry, 128
LPG-powered, 128
braking system for truck-trailers, 138
"piggy-back" service, 146, 153
Fiberglas construction, 147
trunk, 59
trunk racks, 81
Tucker automobile, 114, 117
Tucker Corp., 114, 117, 122
Tucker, Preston, 114
turnpikes, 128, 134, 137, 141, 144
Twin Coach Co., 85

**U**

United Motor Corp., 63
U.S. Army
purchases first electric vehicle, 20
uses trucks in Mexican campaign, 63

U.S. Commerce Dept., Automotive Div. of Foreign and Domestic Commerce, 76
United States Motor Car Corp., 50
U.S. Public Roads Bureau, 11
Universal Products Co., 135
University of Mich., 128, 146
upholstery, 81
use by famous persons, organizations, or for particular purpose, *see specific entries:* President of the U.S.; U.S. Army; circuses, etc.
used cars, 28, 56

**V**

Valiant, 150, 151
valves
intake, mechanically-operated, 31
hydraulically-operated, 93, 122
valve seat inserts, 94
Vanderbilt Cup Race, 35
Viking automobile, 88
Vincent, Jesse G. 64
voltage regulators, 96

**W**

Walker, James B., 23
war production by auto industry
WWI, 60–63
WWII, 108–112
Korean conflict, 124–127
Ward La France Truck Corp., 149
Wardrop, Walter, 46
warranties, 28, 57, 92, 154
Washington Park (Ill.) race, 23
watch, offered as accessory, 126
water pumps, 151
Waterman Arrowbile, 100
Webb, Frank G., 28
Weeks, G. M., 46
Weiss, George L., 21
wheels, 66
wire, 35, 56, 70
solid metal, 60, 70
safety-rim, 106
14-inch wheels, 140
White, Arthur W., 15
White, Walter C., 38, 199
White bus, 33, 94
White Motor Co., 48, 67, 80, 94, 126, 130, 143, 145, 147, 149, 152
White, Rollin, 20

†*Illustration*

White steamer, 32, 48
White truck, 23, 66, 86, 122
Whitman, L. L., 31, 39
Wilkinson, John, 20
Williams Research Co., 150
Wills, C. Harold, 45, 199
Wills Sainte Claire automobile, 83
Willys, John N., 46, 65, 199
Willys Motors, Inc., 104, 136
Willys-Overland vehicles
   Jeepster, 118
   station wagons, 116, 118, 126
   Aero Willys, 127, 136
window lifts, 81
window visors, 93
windows
   power-operated, 115, 117
   retractable rear window, 140
windshield washers, 101
windshield wings, 72
windshield wipers, 63, 77, 85, 106
windshields
   offered as standard equipment, 49, 62

   wrap-around, 56, 134
   slanted, 61, 94
   V-type, 64
   one-piece, 81
   safety glass, 82, 86
   curved, 118, 144
Winton automobile, 17
Winton, Alexander, 17, 20, 201
Winton Motor Carriage Co., 20, 31, 80
Woodall, Charles J., 29

## y

Yellow Truck and Coach Mfg. Co., 81
Yellowstone National Park, admits automobiles, 60

## z

Zachow, Otto, 46
Zeder, Fred M., 72, 77